# Frogs and Toads

**Devin Edmonds**

# Frog and Toads

Project Team
Editor: Thomas Mazorlig
Cover Design: Mary Ann Kahn
Interior Design: Angela Stanford
Indexer: Elizabeth Walker

TFH Publications
President/CEO: Glen S. Axelrod
Executive Vice President: Mark E. Johnson
Publisher: Christopher T. Reggio
Production Manager: Kathy Bontz

TFH Publications, Inc.
One TFH Plaza
Third and Union Avenues
Neptune City, NJ 07753

Printed and bound in China,

06 07 08 09 10  1 3 5 7 9 8 6 4 2

**Library of Congress Cataloging-in-Publication Data**
Edmonds, Devin.
  Frogs and toads / Devin Edmonds.
      p. cm.
  Includes bibliographical references and index.
  ISBN 978-0-7938-2862-3 (alk. paper)
  1. Frogs as pets. 2. Toads as pets.  I. Title.
  SF459.F83E357 2011
  639.3'789--dc22

                          2010024460

*The Leader In Responsible Animal Care For Over 50 Years!*™
www.tfh.com

# Table of Contents

*Agalychnis callidryas*

# Chapter 1

# Frogs and Toads as Pets

**F**rogs and toads are fascinating. There are giant frogs capable of eating snakes and birds, and tiny ones barely larger than a grain of rice. Some can nearly freeze solid, returning to normalcy after being warmed up, while others cope with dry desert habitats by wrapping themselves in a waterproof mucous cocoon to retain moisture. The diverse adaptations amphibians display make them intriguing animals to keep, though the real enjoyment to be had from keeping frogs and toads may lie in their charm. Fairytales tell stories of frog princes who must be kissed, while smiling cartoon frogs can be found advertising products on television. It's no surprise then that these captivating creatures make likeable pets. Just look at a frog's face and I'm sure you'll smile.

Frogs begin life (usually) as aquatic tadpoles, eventually growing limbs, losing the tail, and breathing air. This pig frog (*Rana grylio*) tadpole is well on its way to becoming a frog.

## What Are Frogs and Toads?

Frogs and toads are amphibians, along with salamanders, newts, and caecilians. Nearly 90 percent of amphibian species belong to the order of frogs and toads, collectively known as Anura. Anurans can be told apart from salamanders and newts because adult frogs lack tails and from caecilians because frogs have legs.

The two-part life cycle is what defines amphibians; most species have a larval stage (usually aquatic) and an adult stage. Frogs and toads start life as tadpoles. These aquatic larvae experience dramatic transformation during metamorphosis, when nearly every organ in their bodies changes. Hind limbs develop first, while arms break free from the sides of the body just before leaving the water. During the final stages, frogs and toads stop feeding as the mouth transforms so they can adopt a carnivorous diet. They live off the nutrients provided by the tail as the mouth changes.

The skin of frogs is permeable, allowing them to both breathe and drink through it. The skin is kept moist by mucous glands. Many frogs and toads also have glands that secrete defensive poisons, and their skin may be brightly colored to warn predators of this. Frogs of all imaginable colors exist, including purple-striped *Atelopus* toads and red-dotted poison dart frogs. Most anurans, however, are rather subdued in coloration. This helps them blend into their surroundings to avoid detection.

Vision is important to anurans. Most rely heavily on eyesight to hunt prey and detect predators, though they are effectively blind unless objects around them are moving. The big round spot just behind the eye is called the tympanum and is essentially a large ear drum. They have good hearing as long as sounds are within the frequencies of their own species's call. Frogs and toads vocalize to attract mates and defend territory. In most species, it is the male that calls.

Adaptable and diverse, frogs and toads are found on all continents except Antarctica. They inhabit an array of environments, from temperate wetlands to tropical rainforests. They also live in dry regions of tundra and desert. Some species are fully aquatic, never leaving water after completing metamorphosis. Others spend considerable time burrowed underground. There are also arboreal frogs that breed in tree holes and never set foot on the ground, and the more familiar semi-aquatic frogs which have pond-side homes. The upper Amazon basin has the greatest diversity of species, with its tropical wet climate supporting hundreds of different kinds.

## Taxonomy

The class Amphibia contains more than 6,200 species of frogs, toads, newts, salamanders, and caecilians. Close to 5,600 species are frogs and toads of the order Anura, with more being described by scientists all the time. Organizing all of these species based on their evolutionary relationships into families and genera is an intimidating task, and taxonomists regularly disagree about how this should be done. The largest anuran families include Hylidae (tree frogs), Bufonidae (true toads) and Strabomantidae (South American frogs that lack free-swimming aquatic larvae), each containing more than 500 species.

## Amphibian Population Declines and Extinctions

Scientists have documented alarming declines in frog populations worldwide, with many local populations going extinct altogether. Nearly one third of all

## Is it a Frog or a Toad?

Traditionally, the family Bufonidae has been reserved for the warty-skinned, usually brown, usually terrestrial amphibians commonly known as toads. However, many anuran species also commonly referred to as toads are not in that family. A familiar example is the fire-bellied toad, which is semi-aquatic and green, but nonetheless called a toad. This toad and all others are in fact frogs. An easy way to think about frogs and toads is to remember that all toads are frogs but not all frogs are toads. In this book, "frogs" and "frogs and toads" will be used interchangeably.

amphibian species are threatened with extinction according to the World Conservation Union. While certainly distressing to those of us with an interest in frogs, this is also a huge concern at a larger level, as an entire group of animals representing millions of years of evolution disappears over the course of several decades and the biodiversity of our planet is rapidly diminished.

Many frogs secrete toxic or irritating chemicals when threatened, seen here as the thick white liquid seeping from the parotoid gland of a marine toad.

One of the greatest factors contributing to declining frog and toad populations is habitat destruction. As the human population grows, it consumes more resources, often at a cost to the environment. Agricultural activity, urbanization, logging, and wetland drainage alter or destroy frog and toad habitat. Roads and development may separate populations from one another or from important breeding sites. Habitat protection and management help to offset the damage.

An emerging infectious disease is also threatening frogs and toads. The chytrid fungus *Batrachochytrium dendrobatidis* (Bd for short) was only recently described, but it is causing large problems for the world's amphibians. Once present in an environment, it can wipe out nearly all frogs and toads within several months. It is not clear exactly how this fungus is spreading, but it has now been documented to cause local population crashes and extinctions around the world, even in pristine habitat and protected areas.

How can you help? Get involved with a local conservation organization or frog monitoring project. To avoid introducing foreign pathogens to native frogs and toads, do not release captive amphibians into the wild or dispose of their waste outside (use your household garbage receptacles). Additionally, be aware of the source of a pet amphibian. Exotic or rare wild-caught frogs and toads are best left to experienced breeders and zoological institutions.

# Frogs and Toads as Pets

Hundreds of different kinds of frogs and toads can be found for sale. Some make superb captives and have proven themselves hardy even in the hands of first-time frog owners. Other species are exceedingly sensitive to their environment or stress easily and are best left for experienced keepers. Spend time carefully deciding what species you want to keep, research its care thoroughly, set up the cage, and only after all this is done acquire them.

## Acquiring a Frog

Sources of pet frogs and toads include pet stores, specialist herp dealers ("herp" is the term for reptiles and amphibians collectively), breeders, reptile shows, and collecting from nature. Each source has its own pros and cons.

**Pet Stores** Pet stores regularly stock a few different species. Stores that specialize in exotic animals offer a larger selection. At a pet store you can inspect not only individual frogs to ensure they are healthy before purchase but also the conditions they are kept in. A quality pet store houses different species in separate enclosures. Pet stores can also be a good local source for information, though it's smart to be wary because not every employee is particularly knowledgeable about amphibians.

**Herp Dealers** Herp dealers distribute reptiles and amphibians to the pet trade; they often have low prices and a large selection of species available. These businesses are best located on the Internet or through advertisements in reptile and amphibian magazines. While their prices may be cheap, the cost can be offset once the addition of shipping charges is factored in. Additionally, amphibians are sometimes cared for poorly by dealers, so frogs and toads may arrive in less than prime condition.

**Breeders** It may seem a bit odd that there are people and even businesses that specialize in breeding exotic frogs, but they exist and are the absolute best way to acquire a new anuran pet. Breeders can be located by contacting a local herpetological society, searching the Internet, or attending a reptile show. Breeders offer quality amphibians at good prices and are also a great source for information. Unfortunately, only a handful of species are regularly bred in captivity so you will not be able to find all types of frogs and toads through breeders.

## Saving the Frogs

Conservation organizations have been created to help curb amphibian population declines and extinctions. The Amphibian Specialist Group (www.amphibians. org) is coordinating a global plan to protect wild populations and their associated habitat. Amphibian Ark (www. amphibianark.org) works to establish captive populations of threatened amphibian species in case of extinction.

# The Oldest Frogs

**Many frogs seldom live more than a few years in the wild, but in captivity they can reach a surprisingly old age. The African clawed frog has been recorded as living more than 20 years, while a captive American toad (*Bufo americanus*) survived to an age of 36!**

**Reptile Shows** Reptile shows (also called herp shows and herp expos) are events where herp dealers, breeders, and specialty pet stores bring their animals to show and sell. They are a great place to buy amphibians because prices are cheap, there is often an interesting selection of species, and it's possible to inspect multiple individuals before purchase. To locate a reptile show, check in herp hobbyist magazines or join a local herpetological society.

**Collection** In decades past, collecting a frog or toad from the wild was often the only way to acquire one. Now there are a handful of species that are regularly bred in captivity, and their captive-bred offspring form a better alternative to collecting a frog from the neighborhood pond. But if the species of frog or toad you want to work with is locally abundant and it is not bred in captivity, consider spending a morning in the field to capture one. A permit may be required to collect amphibians in some areas, so check with the proper government agency first. Also, it is especially important to never release a frog back into the wild to avoid harming local amphibian populations.

## Handling

Certain rugged species, such as the marine toad (*Bufo marinus*) and White's tree frog (*Litoria caerulea*), tolerate short periods of handling, but for the most part frogs and toads should be left unhandled. Salts and oils naturally found on human hands irritate the sensitive skin of amphibians. Handling a frog or toad with dry hands can cause severe problems and even death to the animal, so if an anuran must be handled, make sure to do so with wet

Relatively few species of frogs are bred in captivity, but that number continues to grow. Here is a female golden mantella and her eggs.

## Four Good First Frogs

**Oriental fire-bellied toad (*Bombina orientalis*):** With their attractive coloration, diurnal activity, and hardy nature Bombina make superb pets, especially when they are kept in groups.

**African clawed frog (*Xenopus laevis*):** Familiar to both science classrooms and the aquarium trade, this fully aquatic frog has two tiny eyes that seem to always say "Is it dinner time?"

**White's tree frog (*Litoria caerulea*):** This hefty tree frog readily accepts food from a hand and entertains at night when it moves about its arboreal home.

**Ornate horned frog (*Ceratophrys ornata*):** A low-maintenance feeding machine, the ornate horned frog is perfect for those who want an undemanding pet.

hands. Even better is to use a moist fish net or small container to capture the animal. Alternatively, keepers can wear moistened vinyl gloves—unpowdered ones only—to prevent harm.

It should be noted that many frogs and toads have defensive toxins. Because amphibians see us as a threat, they may use their defensive poison while being handled. Always wash your hands thoroughly after handling frogs and toads. There are few species able to cause more harm than minor irritation, but to be safe leave pet frogs and toads alone.

## Acclimation and Quarantine

An important but often overlooked aspect of frog care is the initial period of time directly after acquisition. Be cautious the first month or two a frog is in your care. Observe newly acquired individuals carefully, but do not disturb them unless needed to reduce stress. Health problems seem to develop more often during the first few weeks than they do at any other time due to stress from being transferred and moved around.

Keep newly acquired amphibians in a separate room away from others. Frogs and toads may carry diseases that current pets have no resistance to, or which are deadly, even though a new frog or toad has yet to show symptoms of them. Perform maintenance on the new frogs or toads after doing so with other herps, and consider disinfecting hands and equipment before and after performing care. After a few weeks of this quarantine period, you can feel more confident that the new amphibians are healthy. Many institutions and amphibian breeders quarantine newly acquired animals for 90 days or longer to be safe.

*Ceratophrys cranwelli*

# Chapter 2

# Housing

**W**ith their permeable skin and sensitivity to environmental conditions, frogs and toads need to have their habitats set up with particular care. Don't worry; housing rarely need be complex. By learning about water quality, temperature regulation, and the natural habitat of a frog or toad, setting up the enclosure becomes not only easy but also enjoyable.

Glass aquariums are the most common frog enclosures, and they work for a wide range of species, including the Chacoan horned frog.

## The Enclosure

Glass aquariums are the most common type of housing used for frogs, and for good reason. They are widely available at pet stores and are relatively affordable. Glass is smooth and non-porous, making it easy to clean. Aquariums also offer good visibility. Use a screen cover rather than a glass top to offer ventilation. Homemade combination glass and screen covers can be used instead for species that require high levels of humidity.

In recent years, glass enclosures designed specifically for herps have become widely available through pet stores. With sliding or hinged doors on the front, these cages make maintenance easier and often are better suited than standard aquariums for keeping anurans. Enclosures with access through the front are especially useful when keeping nervous or jumpy species. While front-opening cages may fetch a higher price than standard aquaria, they're usually worth it.

An alternative way to house frogs is in plastic storage containers. These are lightweight, cheap and easily cleaned, and with a little modification they form superb frog homes. To turn a plastic storage container into an amphibian abode, first cut a large hole in the cover. Then place fiberglass window screen over the box and snap the cover back on. Holes can also be drilled into the sides for additional ventilation. The downside to using a storage container for housing is that visibility is reduced. Such containers also melt under heat, so be cautious about where heating devices are placed. Modified plastic storage containers are ideal for simple quarantine setups because they are easy to clean, lightweight, and durable.

## Substrate

The substrate is material that lines the bottom of the enclosure (sometimes called bedding, although many amphibians will not sleep in it). There are many different options. A good substrate holds moisture, is easily cleaned, and is safe if accidentally swallowed or is impossible for an amphibian to ingest. Simple substrates made of inert materials are hygienic and are perfect for maintaining messy frogs and toads. Those composed of more natural materials often look better and may be required for certain species that burrow.

### Paper Towels

A layer of moistened paper towels can work well as a substrate for just about any terrestrial or arboreal frog. Opt for plain brown paper towels because bleached or dyed paper may contain trace amounts of harmful chemicals. Paper towels dry quickly, so be sure to monitor their moisture content. It's also important to replace them frequently—daily if they appear soiled—because if neglected dirty paper towels soon come alive with bacteria.

### Foam Rubber

Available from fabric stores, upholstery foam rubber is a good choice for creating a simple hygienic setup. It is sold in varying thicknesses and sizes, from 0.5 inch (1.3 cm) thick cushions to 8.0 inch (20.3 cm) thick sheets of bed padding. In order for foam rubber to work as a substrate it must stay clean and moist. Rinse it well with hot water to remove feces, dead feeder insects, and other waste, and replace it regularly to avoid harmful bacterial buildup.

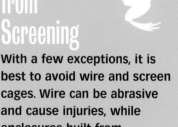

## Stay Away from Screening

With a few exceptions, it is best to avoid wire and screen cages. Wire can be abrasive and cause injuries, while enclosures built from screening dry quickly. Soft fabric-like screen enclosures can work well for certain tree frogs, but for most species it's best to stick with glass or plastic housing.

## Reptile Carpeting and Artificial Turf

While various pet carpet substrates are often recommended for frogs and toads, they can be abrasive and rarely retain moisture well. It is also time consuming to thoroughly clean carpeting. These substrates can work well for frogs and toads from drier environments, though. Choose carpeting that is soft in texture rather than the variety with sharp artificial grass sewn into it. Place patches of moist moss on top of reptile carpet to form humid retreats. It's helpful to have an extra section of carpeting on hand for cleaning. You can place the extra in the cage while you wash the one that was in the cage. When the extra piece is soiled, switch back to the original and clean the extra one.

Plain paper towels are an acceptable substrate for terrestrial frogs, such as this Asian horned frog in a quarantine setup.

## Bare Bottom

In some situations it's advantageous to go without a substrate. Aquatic species are particularly well suited to a bare-bottom setup. This makes cleanup a cinch; just siphon up waste from the floor once a day. Certain tree frogs can also be kept without substrate. This is useful in vertically oriented enclosures that have a drain in the bottom. Waste can then be sprayed out through the drain with a hose to maintain a high level of cleanliness. Terrestrial frogs and toads should not be housed on a bare bottom for extended periods of time.

## Coconut Husk Fiber

A superb substrate for nearly all land-dwelling anurans is coconut husk fiber (also called coir). It's made from the hairy fibers found on coconut shells, which are ground into a soil-like substance and then compressed into a dry brick. The brick can then be soaked in warm water, where it expands back into a moisture-retentive safe substrate for amphibians.

Spot cleaning must be performed regularly so that it does not spoil. Coconut husk fiber has enough moisture for most species when it holds its form when squeezed by hand but is not so wet that water comes pouring out.

## Soil

There are many types of soil available at garden centers. Some can be used successfully with amphibians, but in most situations there are better options available. Potting soil is a particularly poor choice because it contains vermiculite, perlite, fertilizers or other components that can be harmful to frogs and toads. Peat moss can be used with success, but because of its acidic quality and the unsustainable way in which most is collected it is better to use coconut husk fiber instead. Top soil can be a good choice, but the quality of it varies. There is also a risk of introducing parasitic nematode worms and other parasites through the use of soil substrates.

## Moss

With its natural appearance and absorbent properties, moss makes a good substrate. High-quality long-fiber sphagnum moss, which most often is available only from garden centers, is the best kind to use. Take a handful, soak it in water, wring it out, and then pad it down onto the bottom of the enclosure to form a moist, sponge-like substrate. Sphagnum moss has natural antibacterial and antifungal properties adding to its benefits. Green moss found for sale at pet stores can be used to enhance the

Sphagnum moss looks quite natural in a terrarium, and live plants will take root in it.

## Leaf Litter

Many terrestrial frogs and toads appreciate a layer of dried leaves covering part of the substrate. Both oak (*Quercus* spp.) and magnolia (*Magnolia* spp.) leaves are safe to use. Thoroughly dry the leaves for several weeks to reduce the chance of introducing harmful pathogens or pests, and ensure they are collected from an area free of pesticides or other harmful chemicals. Leaves can be boiled or baked in the oven to further reduce the chance of introducing disease.

appearance of an enclosure but should not be used as the sole substrate, because feeder insects often hide in it and it does not pack down very well, posing a risk of accidentally being ingested by frogs and toads.

### Bark and Mulch

At both pet stores and garden centers a wide variety of barks and mulches are available. Several problems can arise when these materials are used as substrate; the most common problem is that pieces are ingested by aggressive feeders. Fir bark and orchid bark mixes should be avoided in most situations for this reason, although when combined with coconut husk fiber, sphagnum moss, or other ingredients they may work well for frogs that do not lunge aggressively at food. Cypress mulch can be used successfully, but because it is manufactured by feeding young cypress trees into wood chippers, consequently destroying wetlands that are important to preserve for wild amphibians, pass it up for other options.

### Gravel and Stones

Gravel and smooth river stones form a good substrate for semi-aquatic and aquatic frogs. Many sizes are available from pet stores. Choose a grade of stone that is too large to easily be swallowed. Before use, always rinse gravel to remove debris. When designing terrestrial setups, gravel can be used as a base layer for excess water to drain into underneath sphagnum moss, coconut husk fiber, or soil. Use a layer of fiberglass window screen to separate the layers, and siphon excess water from the gravel before the water approaches the substrate above it. Gravel should not be used alone for terrestrial frogs and toads; it does not hold moisture, can cause problems if swallowed, and is abrasive.

### Sand

Although sand is readily available at pet stores, avoid using it in most setups. For aquatic species, fine-grade sand safe for freshwater aquariums can be used instead of gravel,

# Table 1: Good Plants for Frog Terrariums

| Scientific Name | Common Name | Comments |
|---|---|---|
| *Aglaonema* spp. | Chinese Evergreen | Will outgrow small cages |
| *Alocasia* spp. | Elephant Ear | Attractive foliage, dwarf varieties are best |
| *Anthurium* spp. | Anthurium | Many available species, most grow quite large |
| *Anubias barteri* | Anubias | Sold as an aquatic, but great when grown with leaves out of water |
| *Asplenium* spp. | Bird's Nest Fern | Strong supportive leaves, but outgrows small enclosures |
| *Calathea* spp. | Calathea | Leaves support tree frogs well, hardy |
| *Cryptanthus* spp. | Earth Star | Needs well-drained soil |
| *Elodea* spp. | Anacharis | Hardy aquatic plant |
| *Ficus pumila* | Creeping Fig | Fast-growing vine, requires high humidity levels |
| *Fittonia* spp. | Polk-a-Dot Plant | May be trampled by large frogs |
| *Guzmania* spp. | Bromeliad | Needs well-drained soil or can be grown epiphytically |
| *Limnobium laevigatum* | Amazon Frogbit | Floating plant grown on surface of water |
| *Maranta* spp. | Prayer Plant | Prefers high humidity levels |
| *Myriophyllum aquaticum* | Parrot's Feather | Aquatic plant that sends up frilly shoots above water |
| *Neoregelia* spp. | Bromeliad | Needs well-drained soil or can be grown epiphytically |
| *Pellionia pulchra* | Satin Pellionia | Attractive, fast-growing vine |
| *Pilea* spp. | Aluminum Plant | May be trampled by large frogs, grows quickly |
| *Philodendron* spp. | Philodendron | Excellent terrarium plants, many species available |
| *Salvinia molesta* | Giant Salvinia | Floating plant grown on surface of water |
| *Sansevieria trifasciata* | Snake Plant | Needs well-drained soil, will outgrow small enclosures |
| *Scindapsus aureus* | Pothos | Hardy plant that grows quickly, prune frequently |
| *Scindapsus pictus* | Silver Vine | Attractive foliage, a slower-growing alternative to pothos |
| *Spathiphyllum* spp. | Peace Lily | Great as emergent vegetation in water |
| *Syngonium podophyllum* | Arrowhead Vine | Hardy, grows quickly |
| *Tradescantia fluminensis* | Wandering Jew | Fast-growing colorful vine |
| *Verisicularia dubyana* | Java Moss | Great when placed at water's edge, looks like moss |
| *Vriesea* spp. | Bromeliad | Needs well-drained soil or can be grown epiphytically |

# Impaction

**Substrates that are easily swallowed but are difficult for frogs and toads to pass can cause dangerous impactions. Pea gravel, loose moss, and fir bark are particularly risky substrates to use for aggressive feeders prone to swallowing substrate with food.**

though it may be difficult to clean. Sand is also useful for certain burrowing species when it's mixed with coconut husk fiber or soil.

## Cage Furnishings

Driftwood, cork bark, artificial or live plants, and commercially available hide spots can all be used to furnish an enclosure for frogs or toads. These items create microclimates within a cage. If the humidity level falls, frogs and toads may burrow into the substrate under a piece of bark where there is more moisture. Many tree frogs climb plants or driftwood to move closer to lighting where it is warmer. Keep in mind the species of frog or toad you plan to keep while furnishing the cage in order to accommodate its particular needs. Cage items also provide a sense of security to captive amphibians and create visual barriers, which are important when keeping a group of frogs or toads together.

### Live Plants

Live plants are an excellent way to provide cover in an aesthetically pleasing way. Wash all live plants thoroughly before use. If you suspect they have been exposed to chemicals that could be harmful to amphibians (leaf shiners, fertilizers, etc.), grow plants outside the cage for several weeks before putting them into the enclosure. It's also important to replant them in a soil that is safe for amphibians—one that does not contain perlite, vermiculite, or fertilizers. Coconut husk fiber may work well for this purpose. In some setups, it's possible to replant plants in the substrate of the cage; burrowing amphibians, however, may uproot plants. Note that even though frogs and toads may not require special lighting, most live plants need a fluorescent bulb or two running the length of the enclosure in order to thrive.

### Backgrounds

For nervous or active species, consider using a background to reduce stress. The simplest background is a piece of paper taped to three outer sides of the enclosure. This helps prevent jumpy species from trying to escape through glass, which can result in injury. Alternatively, cork bark, tree fern panels, or commercially available terrarium backgrounds can be attached to the inside of an enclosure with aquarium-safe silicone sealant. This should be done before adding substrate or other furnishings. Do not introduce frogs or toads until the enclosure no longer smells strongly of silicone sealant, which takes several days.

## Water Sources and Quality

A crucial aspect of housing frogs and toads is providing access to a source of clean fresh water. For terrestrial species, this may be as simple as placing a small water dish in the enclosure. The dish should be easy to access, for both you and your frogs. The water dish may need to be changed daily. Aquatic frogs and toads require a setup more like an aquarium for fish, where water quality is maintained through filtration and frequent partial water changes.

Choose your water source carefully. Aged tap water can be used but must first be treated with an aquarium water conditioner that removes chlorine and chloramines and neutralizes heavy metals. Test tap water for pH and general hardness to further ensure it is safe for amphibians. Many pet stores do this for free if you bring them a water sample. If tap water is unsafe for use, distilled or reverse osmosis (RO) water can be used instead but must first have essential salts and minerals added back into it so that it isn't too pure. Well water varies greatly in quality and must be tested for pH, hardness, and nitrates before use.

### Chlorine and Chloramines

Municipalities add chlorine or chloramines to tap water in order to kill pathogens. While safe for humans, both chemicals are toxic to amphibians. Chlorine evaporates rather quickly (in about 24 hours in an uncovered container), but these days most cities use chloramines, which must be removed with an aquarium water conditioner. To be safe, always condition tap water and age it for at least one day before use.

African dwarf frogs and other aquatic frogs fare well on a substrate of large gravel and/or smooth river stones.

## Water Hardness and pH

Water hardness is a measure of mineral content in water, especially calcium and magnesium—hard water has more dissolved minerals than soft water. The hardness of water is related to pH, a measure of acidity or alkalinity. Test kits are available at pet stores to measure both of these properties, but generally the two do not fluctuate widely, so it's only necessary to test for them at first to determine whether a source of water is safe for amphibians. Hard water can be diluted with distilled or RO water to make it safe.

Live plants provide frogs with hiding places and, in aquatic enclosures, help to maintain the water quality.

A pH between 6.0 and 8.0 is suitable for most captive frogs and toads, but it's important that the pH stays stable and does not fluctuate quickly. Avoid using chemical aquarium additives to alter pH, because they can cause dangerous swings in water quality. Instead, if water has a pH outside the safe range, consider finding a new water source.

## Dissolved Gases

When coming out of a pressurized pipe, water is often saturated with dissolved gases like nitrogen and carbon dioxide. This can cause health problems for amphibians. Allow water to stand in an open-topped container for 24 hours so that gases dissipate, making it safe for frogs and toads. Agitating the water helps to speed up the dissipation process.

# Maintaining Water Quality and the Nitrogen Cycle

When using small volumes of water, such as in a water dish, the best way to keep it clean is to replace it daily. Keep a jug of amphibian-safe water prepped and ready to refill dishes with.

For semi-aquatic and aquatic species, maintaining water quality can be a bit more complicated because of the larger volume of water involved. Fortunately, it's not entirely up to you to keep the water clean. Given time, beneficial nitrifying bacteria can become established and help to control waste produced by frogs and toads. Performing regular partial water changes (30 percent every other week is usually suitable) will keep semi-aquatic or aquatic environments safe for anurans. Replacing too much water at once can shock amphibians and hurt beneficial bacteria. Normally it's best to change half or less of the water at once.

Ammonia ($NH_3$) is naturally formed in aquaria from organic waste breaking down. This compound is extremely toxic to amphibians. In an established aquatic environment with a healthy population of beneficial bacteria, ammonia is immediately turned into nitrite ($NO_2$)—still dangerous but slightly less harmful than ammonia. As nitrite is formed, a second type of bacteria feed on it and produce nitrate ($NO_3$), which is relatively harmless to amphibians at low levels (below 20 parts per million). The goal when keeping aquatic or semi-aquatic frogs is to maintain a healthy population of beneficial nitrifying bacteria that immediately convert dangerous ammonia into nitrite and nitrite into the less dangerous nitrate, which is then removed with partial water changes.

## Making Water

Sometimes tap water is not safe to use because it is too hard or is suspected of containing heavy metals. In these situations, consider mixing up your own frog water. Start with reverse osmosis or distilled water purchased from the grocery store. Then mix in an aquarium product designed to add the appropriate amount of salts and trace elements to these pure water sources.

## Filtration

In addition to performing frequent partial water changes, filtration helps maintain water quality, although it is not always necessary. Filters provide three functions. They mechanically collect waste and particles in the water column, chemically improve water quality, and provide surface area for beneficial bacteria to grow on.

Placing some stones in the water bowl can help prevent small species, such as the western green toad, from drowning by giving them a way to climb out of the water.

## The Right Rock for the Job

**Not all rocks are safe to use as cage furnishings. Some can adversely affect water quality. Don't use marble, limestone, or anything with a metallic shine, and instead play it safe by sticking with slate, granite or quartz.**

**Sponge Filters** Sponge filters are an inexpensive, low-tech method of filtration; they have been used for decades. They are especially good for use in aquariums housing tadpoles. Sponge filters operate by drawing water through a sponge that collects some floating particulate waste but not large waste particles; the main purpose of a sponge filter is to harbor colonies of beneficial bacteria. Sponge filters' most common method of operation is to be powered by an air pump that moves air through a tube in the middle of the sponge, creating a flow through the filter. Maintenance involves rinsing the sponge weekly. Sponge filters do not chemically filter water and are best for small aquariums.

**Power Filters** A particularly effective way to filter water is with a power filter. Two styles of relatively inexpensive power filters are available: submersible ones that sit underwater inside the tank and hang-on-the-tank filters that sit outside the aquarium over the back. Filtration media vary, but they usually incorporate carbon to chemically remove dissolved organic wastes, odors, and discoloration. Carbon must be replaced monthly. Use submersible power filters in semi-aquatic setups where moderate volumes of water need to be filtered, and power filters that hang on the tank for filtering fully aquatic setups with larger volumes of water.

**Undergravel Filters** Undergravel filters work by drawing waste down through gravel in an aquarium, where beneficial bacteria help break it down. In the average aquatic frog tank too much waste is produced for this system to work effectively. Use undergravel filtration only if other types of filters aren't available, and pay close attention to the filter plates beneath the gravel to ensure excess waste does not build up beneath them. In my opinion, it's best to pass up undergravel filters for other options.

**Canister Filters** Canister filters sit underneath aquaria, with an input and output tube running up from below. Water is drawn in and forced through various types of filtration media depending on what is placed inside the canister. Canister filters are overkill for small aquaria, but for tanks larger than 30 gallons (114 l) they may be the best option.

## Cleaning and Maintenance

Maintaining a clean environment for captive frogs is among the most important parts of their care. Waste, such as dead feeder insects or feces, should be spot cleaned as it is noticed. How often the substrate is replaced and cage items are cleaned depends on the material, size of the enclosure, and how many animals are being kept.

Paper towels, foam rubber, and cage carpeting should be cleaned or replaced frequently, up to several times a week. A layer of moist sphagnum moss or coconut husk fiber, on the other hand, may only need to be changed every few months in a lightly stocked tank that is spot cleaned frequently. The smell of a cage is a good way to determine whether it needs to be cleaned. It should never smell swampy or sour; rather it should smell fresh and pleasantly organic, like a garden or the forest floor.

In aquatic and semi-aquatic setups maintenance involves frequent partial water changes. To avoid harming beneficial bacteria, never take the gravel out of the aquarium and rinse it. Instead, use an aquarium vacuum while performing water changes to lift excess waste from the gravel. A small siphon or turkey baster can be used to suck up leftover food and waste between water changes.

Avoid using chemicals to clean enclosures that house amphibians. Frogs and toads have permeable skin and are especially sensitive to soaps and detergents. Hot tap water usually does the job just fine. White vinegar and a razor blade are especially helpful for removing water spots from glass.

If a frog or toad needs to be medicated or is sick, it may be necessary to disinfect the enclosure. To do this, first clean all material from the cage with hot water and dispose of organic cage items that cannot be sterilized (the substrate, driftwood, live plants, etc.) Then use a 10-percent bleach solution to clean the cage, water dish, artificial plants, and décor. Allow the cage and cage items to sit in this solution for at least 10 minutes, then rinse until they do not smell of bleach. You can soak everything in water with an aquarium water conditioner at twice the recommended strength to

### Cleaning the Responsible Way

Discard substrate, waste, and used cage items in a responsible way. To avoid exposing wild amphibian populations to pathogens captive frogs may carry, never throw such discarded items into the outside environment.

Incandescent lights are the most common method for heating frog enclosures. Live plants often require additional lighting.

chemically neutralize any residual bleach afterwards. Let everything air dry thoroughly before reuse.

## Temperature Regulation

Frogs and toads are found all over the world, so it's no surprise that different species require different temperatures in captivity. Many anurans are sensitive to warm temperatures, and very few require or tolerate those above 90°F (32.2°C). Similarly, there are many tropical frogs and toads that should not be exposed to cool conditions below 60°F (15.6°C). In order to regulate the temperature effectively, first the preferred temperature range of the species must be known, then the temperature in the cage should be measured with an accurate thermometer, and finally heating or cooling devices should be added if necessary.

Thermometer strips that stick to the side of an enclosure are not useful because they measure the temperature of the glass or plastic they are attached to rather than the temperatures inside the cage. Opt for plastic thermometers with suction cups that can be moved around inside the enclosure. Digital thermometers with external probes are an even better choice.

### Heating

If heating is needed, one of the easiest ways to adjust the temperature is with lighting. Incandescent light bulbs can be positioned above a screen cover for heating. Special ones made of red or black glass are ideal because they can be left on overnight, not only providing heat but also offering a view of nocturnal activity. Only in very large enclosures are powerful light bulbs needed, and most often a 25- to 75-watt bulb will do the job. Fluorescent light bulbs produce little heat compared to incandescent ones, but in some situations a fluorescent strip light may be all that is needed to warm a cage by several degrees.

Herp heating pads can be used instead of light bulbs to warm amphibian cages. Some brands may get too hot for use with frogs and toads, so take care when choosing one. For burrowing species, place heat pads on the side rather than underneath the tank. If using a thick layer of substrate, opt for heating from above with a light instead of with a heating pad.

In aquatic and semi-aquatic setups, use a fully submersible aquarium heater to heat the water. Choose one with a built-in thermostat that allows you to set the temperature exactly. Even with this type of heater, check the temperature daily.

## Cooling

Cooling an enclosure is more difficult than heating one, but it can be necessary during some summer days or when simulating a winter period to induce breeding. The easiest option is to move the cage to an air conditioned room, basement, or other cool location. Positioning a small fan over water in a semi-aquatic or aquatic setup can decrease the temperature by several degrees as well. Evaporation has a cooling effect, so in addition to placing a fan over water you can also mist an enclosure to briefly cool it in an emergency. Another simple way to cool an overly warm tank on a hot day is to unplug all lights, filters, heaters, and other electrical devices that produce heat. This may seem a bit obvious, but it is often overlooked.

## Humidity

Humidity is a measure of water vapor in the air. Because frogs and toads have permeable skin that must stay moist, the humidity inside the enclosure is an important consideration.

# Different Species; Different Enclosures

Housing multiple species together rarely works in the long term. Most difficult is providing different environments within the same enclosure that are safe for all inhabitants. Many frogs also will eat smaller amphibians or bully others out of food. Perhaps the greatest but an often ignored risk involved when housing multiple species together is that of disease. Species from different sources or different parts of the world often harbor pathogens other amphibians have no resistance to. Keep your frogs and toads in prime condition by keeping each species in its own enclosure.

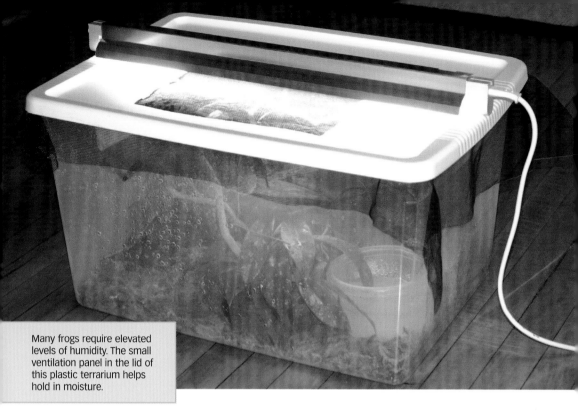

Many frogs require elevated levels of humidity. The small ventilation panel in the lid of this plastic terrarium helps hold in moisture.

Average household humidity levels (35 to 60 percent) are fine for many frogs and toads, but species from tropical environments require higher levels of humidity. An easy way to increase humidity is to mist a cage with a spray bottle once or twice a day. Providing plenty of surfaces on which water droplets can gather helps maintain humid conditions following misting. Remember to use only aged chlorine-free water. Reverse osmosis water or distilled water purchased from a grocery store can be used to prevent water spots from developing on glass.

Restricting ventilation is another way to increase humidity. Plastic wrap or a piece of glass can be taped over part of a screen cover. Take care not to seal up too much of the cage because providing good ventilation can be even more important than maintaining humid conditions.

## Lighting

Lighting serves several purposes. Most important, it provides a photoperiod so that there is a difference between day and night. Keep lights on for 10 to 12 hours each day. Lighting also provides heat, which may or may not be necessary. Lastly, certain light bulbs produce ultraviolet (UV) radiation. Using a light bulb with the proper spectrum of UV rays may be beneficial to certain anurans that are regularly exposed to the sun in nature. While amphibians do not require access to UVB radiation, as many reptiles do, it does not hurt to provide a small amount in one area of the enclosure. If you plan on providing UVB radiation to frogs, pick a light bulb that emits around 2 percent to avoid offering too much. UVB-producing light bulbs should be replaced every six to eight months and positioned over a screen section of the cover—glass blocks most UV. Consider plugging day lights into an electrical timer so that they are on for between 10 and 12 hours. This way, lights turn on and off at the same time each day.

To improve the appearance of a frog or toad setup, run a fluorescent strip light across the length of the enclosure. This also allows live plants to be grown and ensures the appropriate photoperiod is provided. The color spectrum of the bulb has a large effect on the way the cage looks. Fluorescent bulbs with a color temperature between 5000K and 6500K tend to look most natural, providing crisp white light.

## Examples of Frog and Toad Habitats

There are about as many ways to house frogs and toads as there are people who keep them. Below are just a few ways to set up terrestrial and semi-aquatic environments for amphibians, which should be adjusted to suit the needs of the particular species being kept.

One way to create a semi-aquatic terrarium is to use a piece of glass or Plexiglas to divide the land and water sections. Use silicone aquarium sealant to fix the divider in place as seen here.

### The Simple Setup

A basic but practical setup consists of an aquarium, screen cover, sphagnum moss substrate, water dish, and several hide spots. This style of housing can be modified to work well for many different species, from tree frogs to burrowing toads.

First, place sphagnum moss in amphibian-safe water and wait for it to become saturated. Wring it out until it feels moist, not wet, and then pad it down on the bottom of the aquarium. A layer at least 2.0 inches (5.1 cm) deep should be provided for burrowing species. Arboreal frogs require only a thin layer to cushion the bottom and collect waste. Submerge a water dish into the sphagnum moss towards one end of the cage and then place a couple pieces of cork bark, driftwood, or an artificial plant towards the other. Remember, the goal of these decorations is not only to provide cover but also to provide varying microhabitats within the enclosure (example: moist hide spot, warm basking area, etc.). Add a screen top, a thermometer, and a heating device if necessary, and the setup is complete.

Semi-aquatic terrarium with cork bark divider and live plants suitable for small *Rana* species and fire-bellied toads.

Daily maintenance of this simple setup involves spot cleaning waste and changing the water dish. Sphagnum moss can last for several months or may need to be replaced every two weeks depending on how heavily stocked the enclosure is and how thoroughly you spot clean it. Pay attention to the color and smell of the moss. When sphagnum moss starts looking dark in color or has an unpleasant odor, it's time for a cage cleaning.

## The River's Edge

Housing semi-aquatic amphibians poses a bit of a dilemma because they must have both a land area and a substantial body of water. A simple setup like the one described previously but with a large water dish can work well, but a more attractive form of housing using gravel, some large river stones, and a few plants can be used instead.

Start by filling an aquarium with around 3.0 inches (7.6 cm) of gravel. Slope the gravel towards one end of the tank and then use an object to hold this in place. Large river rocks, cork bark flats, or tree fern slabs can be used for this purpose. The aquarium should now have one end with about 1.0 inch (2.5 cm) of gravel and another end with around 5.0 inches (12.7 cm). This higher end forms the land area.

Fill the aquarium with amphibian-safe water until the water line is just below the top of the gravel on the land area. Cover this with a section of fiberglass window screen. Finally, add a layer of moist sphagnum moss or coconut husk fiber over the screen, keeping this last substrate layer in place with additional river rocks or cork bark. Hardy tropical plants can be grown in the land area and aquatic or emergent species in the water. Their roots help hold the bottom layer of gravel in place so that it does not flatten over time.

Perform partial water changes on a regular basis. A submersible power filter can be used to help maintain water quality in this style of housing. Occasionally the sphagnum moss or coconut husk fiber that covers the land area will need to be replaced, but if waste is removed regularly this may only need to be done every other month or less frequently.

## The Living Terrarium

Thoughtful driftwood structures and delicate plants add flavor to the average frog cage, and with some careful planning a terrarium housing frogs or toads can become the beautiful centerpiece of a room. Terraria are not

**top**: Intermediate stage in the completion of a living terrarium with an aquatic section. The background and LECA drainage layer is in place. A piece of cork bark separates the land and water sections.
**bottom**: In the finished terrarium, the LECA has been covered by a layer of sphagnum moss and leaf litter. The plants are growing directly in the substrate.

only aesthetically pleasing but also easy to maintain, with plants and microorganisms helping break down waste as it forms.

To create a living terrarium, start with an enclosure at least the size of a standard 20-gallon (76 l) aquarium. Consider attaching a background of cork bark or tree fern panels to provide an additional surface for plants to grow on. The substrate must be layered to provide drainage, preventing both plants and frogs from sitting in soggy soil. Use a drainage layer of either aquarium gravel or LECA (lightweight expanded clay aggregate) that is about 2.0 inches (5.1 cm) deep. LECA is preferable because it does not weigh as much as gravel, though it may be difficult to find for sale in some areas. Check with hydroponic supply companies and specialty pet stores.

Over the drainage substrate, place a piece of fiberglass window screen or plastic mesh that measures the footprint of the enclosure. This prevents substrate layers from mixing together. On top of the mesh, pour in a substrate that is safe for amphibians but will support plant growth. Coconut husk fiber mixed with milled sphagnum moss and orchid bark in a 2:1:1 ratio works well.

Once the background and substrate are in place, it's time to add driftwood, cork bark, or other structures. Stick with one type of wood to achieve a natural look, and take time hunting for the right piece. Complex arrangements of driftwood give terraria dramatic form, while a cork bark tube wedged in place above ground provides an attractive perch for arboreal frogs.

Natural terrarium planted with bromeliads, creeping fig, and Java moss. It is suitable for tropical tree frogs or small terrestrial species.

Semi-aquatic living terrarium with an impressive driftwood structure, inhabited by a Fowler's toad (*Bufo fowleri*). A number of ranids would fare well in this type of terrarium.

The best plants for terraria are located on the Internet through terrarium supply companies. See Table 1 for a list of recommended species. Remember to wash plants thoroughly under tap water before use, allowing them to grow outside the enclosure for several weeks if you suspect chemicals such as leaf shiners have been used on them.

To complete a terrarium, add a water dish in an easily accessible spot. Alternatively, a corner of the substrates can be held back with a piece of cork bark or several stones, and then water can be added to the tank until it gathers in this area.

It is important to allow terraria to grow for several weeks before introducing frogs or toads. This gives plants time to root themselves in place. Terrarium maintenance involves the usual spot cleaning, but unlike as with a simple setup, the entire substrate should not be replaced. Microorganisms that live in the substrate help break down waste, and as long as a balance is maintained between the bacteria and waste, the substrate mixture never needs to be entirely replaced. To prevent the substrate from becoming waterlogged, siphon out excess water as it builds up in the drainage layer of gravel or LECA.

*Lepidobatrachus laevis*

# Feeding

Some frogs and toads are picky eaters, feeding almost exclusively on one type of food like termites or other frogs. Many more eat just about any creature that catches their attention and fits into their mouths. In captivity, live invertebrates make up the majority of the diet, although some species also accept pre-killed food from forceps. Understand the dietary requirements of the species you keep as well as the nutritional content of different foods to help ensure a long, healthy life for your frogs and toads.

## Types of Food

### Crickets

The house cricket (*Acheta domestica*) is the most common food item used to feed frogs and toads. House crickets are readily available from pet stores in several sizes or can be ordered in bulk from cricket breeders. For most species, it's best to offer crickets that are about as long as the width of the frog's head. When well fed prior to being used as food, crickets are a relatively healthy meal. They can be used as a staple diet, with other food items being substituted for crickets every few feedings.

Most frogs, including fire-bellied toads, readily accept crickets as food. Make sure the crickets are the appropriate size for your frog.

While it may be unappealing to keep insects in the house, the reality is that if you keep frogs or toads you will also need to keep crickets. Fortunately, they are not difficult to care for. Maintain crickets in a well-ventilated enclosure, such as an aquarium with a screen cover or a plastic container outfitted with aluminum mesh vents. Crickets must be kept warm, with a temperature between 75°F and 80°F (23.9° and 26.7°C) being ideal. At these temperatures, crickets have a life span of over two months, but if adult crickets are being used they may live for only a couple of weeks after acquisition before expiring.

Crickets must have access to fresh food and water to live. This is important for the crickets as well as for the frogs. Starved crickets have little nutritional content, so feed crickets a healthy diet for at least two days before offering them to anurans. Sliced oranges, grapefruit, grapes, carrot, sweet potato, squash, zucchini, collard greens, and dark lettuces keep crickets alive and full of vitamins for when they are ingested by a hungry frog or toad. In addition to these fruits and vegetables, provide a small dish of dry food. Dry cricket diets are available at pet stores; otherwise flake fish food, dry dog food, or rice baby cereal can be used. Replace food every other day or when it appears old. Avoid offering a dish of water, because crickets are prone to drowning. Instead, ensure that there are always fresh fruits and vegetables available to keep crickets hydrated, or moisten a small sponge for drinking.

## Cockroaches

In recent years, various roaches have become popular as frog food. They are easily cultured and can be used alongside crickets as the main dietary component. Don't worry; these roaches are not your average pest roaches. Four species are most often available and come from tropical climates, requiring warm temperatures between 80°F and 95°F (26.7° and 35°C) and high levels of humidity in order to thrive and reproduce.

The lobster roach (*Nauphoeta cinerea*) and Turkistan roach (*Blatta lateralis*) grow about as large as an adult house cricket, while the discoid (*Blaberus discoidalis*) and Guyana orange-spotted (*Blaptica dubia*) roaches grow up to 2.0 inches (5.1 cm) in length. None of these species fly, but lobster roaches can climb, so use a tight-fitting cover on their enclosure to prevent escapes.

Roaches can be kept in an aquarium with a screen cover. Attach a heating pad to the glass so that it stays within the appropriate temperature range. If it's too cool, roaches won't breed. A substrate of coconut husk fiber or sphagnum moss helps maintain high levels of humidity. In addition, add several pieces of cardboard or cork bark and a shallow feeding dish. As with crickets, the food that is fed to cockroaches greatly affects their nutritional content. Use a similar assortment of fresh fruits and vegetables as you would feed to crickets, along with dry dog food, fish flakes, or oats.

## When Predators Become Prey

Uneaten stray crickets have been known to bite frogs and toads. The resulting wound can lead to a serious infection. Even if the wound is not serious, crickets moving over and chewing on your amphibians causes them a lot of stress. Take care to monitor how many crickets are eaten and ensure that there aren't any excess ones roaming the cage in the hours following feeding.

## Earthworms and Night Crawlers

Worms are one of the healthiest foods available for captive frogs and toads. They can be purchased from bait stores or specialty pet stores and offered to amphibians either with forceps or placed in a small feeding bowl.

Several types of worms are available. Whole night crawlers (*Lumbricus terrestris*) are a perfect food to feed large frogs and toads, or they can be cut into pieces for

Tropical roaches make excellent food for frogs and are highly unlikely to infest the house if they escape. This is the Guyana orange-spotted roach.

smaller species. Store night crawlers in the refrigerator at a temperature near 40°F (4.4°C) and they will last for weeks. Red worms (*Eisenia foetida*), also called red wigglers or dung worms, can also be used as food. There is some concern, however, about their safety as a food source because their coelomic fluids may be toxic. A safer alternative to red worms is leaf worms (*Lumbricus rubellus*), which are slightly larger and highly nutritious. If moved to a ventilated container containing top soil, stored in a cool location between 40°F and 60°F (4.4 and 15.5°C), and offered food such as veggies or leaf compost, red worms and leaf worms will survive for months and may even reproduce.

Western toad (*Bufo boreas*) devouring an earthworm. Worms are among the most nutritious foods for frogs.

## Mealworms and Superworms

Larvae of two different tenebrionid beetles are regularly available from pet stores. Both are high in fat and have an exoskeleton that can be difficult to digest, so use them in moderation. Mealworms are the smaller of the two and should be fed to frogs in a feeding dish. Keep mealworms in a container of oatmeal or wheat germ in the refrigerator so that they do not pupate into beetles, and provide them with a slice of apple, sweet potato, or similar food. Superworms, also known as king mealworms, are suitable only for large frogs and toads and are best fed individually to amphibians with forceps. Maintain superworms at room temperature but otherwise like mealworms.

## Wax Worms

Larvae of the wax moth (*Galleria mellonella*) are widely available from pet stores and bait shops. They lack the hard exoskeleton of mealworms and superworms but are even higher in fat. Wax worms are great for bulking up underweight individuals or to feed frogs in preparation for breeding. Store wax worms in the refrigerator to lengthen their larval stage. You can also place them in a ventilated jar at room temperature and allow wax worms to pupate into moths, which can then be fed to tree frogs.

## Houseflies

Found for sale in their larval stage as "spikes" from bait stores or in bulk from feeder insect companies, houseflies (*Musca domestica*) are a great food to feed arboreal frogs and toads. Transfer maggots from the cup they are sold in to a ventilated but secure container, and then keep them at room temperature for several days. Soon maggots pupate, and once the container is buzzing with flies it can be moved to the refrigerator. At cool temperatures flies remain motionless and can easily be tapped into a cage. Once they warm up they begin to fly again; they are perfect for feeding tree frogs.

## Field Sweepings and Wild-Caught Foods

Armed with a fine net and plastic bag, you may be able to capture a wide variety of live foods outside. Katydids, grasshoppers, field crickets, small spiders, and various grubs all provide necessary variety to a captive amphibian diet. An easy method for collecting large quantities of live invertebrates is called field sweeping. Take a fine net to a field and repeatedly run it through tall grass to easily capture prey.

Be cautious about where insects are collected. There is a risk of having pesticides or other harmful contaminants introduced through wild-caught food. Avoid collecting near agricultural fields for this reason. Also, wild-caught food will undoubtedly harbor parasites, which will be introduced to captive frogs or toads. These drawbacks may present problems down the line, so weigh the pros and cons carefully before heading out to catch a bagful of bugs.

## Rodents

Frozen mice and rats are sold at pet stores in various sizes. Large amphibians readily accept freshly thawed rat pups or adult mice when offered with forceps, while smaller species can be fed neonate mice called "pinky mice" due to their hairless pink skin. Take care to use rodents as food only occasionally, because they are high in fat. Also, do not use live rodents; they can bite and injure a frog while being consumed.

## The Other "Worms"

Many other insect larvae are available to the herpetoculturist looking to add variety to a captive amphibian's diet. These include silkworms, butter worms, phoenix worms, tomato hornworms, and bloodworms, among others. You can locate them through special feeder insect companies on the Internet or at herp shows. Silkworms are an especially notable food because of their high nutritional content.

Although large frogs, such as the horned frogs, readily eat rodents, they should be fed sparingly because mice are high in fat.

### Fish

Several types of fish are available from pet stores for use as amphibian food. They can either be introduced to an aquatic setup or fed with forceps to terrestrial species. Use feeder fish only occasionally. If relied upon as the main dietary component, nutritional disorders will likely result. Feeder fish may also introduce ectoparasites to aquatic frogs and their larvae, such as fish lice or anchor worms, so always examine fish carefully before introducing them to an aquarium.

### Blackworms

Used most often to feed tropical fish, live blackworms (*Lumbriculus variegatus*) can also be fed to aquatic frogs and predatory tadpoles. They are available at pet stores and must be stored in the refrigerator. It's important to rinse blackworms thoroughly with cool water daily so that they do not spoil. Blackworms have in many areas replaced tubifex worms as the most commonly offered live food sold in pet and aquarium specialty stores, but tubifex worms are still widely available.

## Food for Tiny Frogs

Feeding small species or baby frogs requires a supply of tiny invertebrates. There are a number of options, though they may take a bit of work to locate or culture. Flightless fruit flies

(*Drosophila* spp.) are the most easily acquired option. Two species are regularly available, *D. melanogaster* and *D. hydei*, with the first reaching only one-sixteenth of an inch (1.6 mm) and the second growing about twice that size. Sometimes fruit flies can be found at pet stores, but the best and most productive fruit fly cultures are ordered online from feeder insect companies.

"Pinhead crickets" are freshly hatched house crickets, and at this age are literally about the size of a pinhead. While pet stores do not regularly carry them, most stores can special order hatchling crickets in bulk if requested. Care is the same as for older crickets, although pinheads tend to be a bit more sensitive, with high mortality occurring when food runs out or when kept at cool temperatures.

For the smallest of frogs, springtails (Collembola) will need to be cultured. Springtails can be acquired at herp shows or from feeder insect companies. Culture springtails on moist charcoal with 0.5 inches (1.3 cm) of water in the bottom, feeding baker's yeast or fish flake at least once a week. To harvest springtails from a culture, remove a piece of charcoal and blow them off into a cage. Alternatively, you may be able to culture springtails in containers with moist coconut husk fiber, which can be spooned out along with the springtails living in it and fed to tiny amphibians.

There are also many wild foods that can be fed to small anurans. One strategy for harvesting tiny invertebrates is to take a handful of moist leaf litter, place it in a fine-mesh kitchen strainer sitting over a bucket, suspend a light bulb above this, and then shake out prey from the leaves. The heat produced by the light bulb directs live foods towards the bottom of the strainer so they can easily be shaken into the bucket below.

## Feeding Frequency and Techniques

How often frogs and toads are fed depends on many factors. Some species have particularly high metabolic rates and require daily feedings. Others only need a large worm or two once a week. Temperature plays an important role in feeding frequency too. Frogs and toads require more food when kept warm than they do when cool. It's also necessary to take note of how much is being fed at each feeding. It is best to feed no more than a frog can eat within a couple of hours of being fed. If fed heavily at one feeding, consider waiting an extra couple days before offering more food. Growing young frogs and toads of all species are best fed in small amounts every 24 hours.

## Feed at Night

**Many frogs and toads are nocturnal. Offer food at night when they are active and ready to eat. This allows the frogs to find and eat their food before the insects groom the supplements off their bodies.**

There are a number of ways to feed frogs and toads. The easiest is to simply release prey into the enclosure. This works well in many situations, though sometimes prey is able to evade hungry pets. It also can become impossible to monitor how much an individual is eating if feeders are simply released into a cage.

To resolve these issues, a feeding dish can be used. Use a smooth-sided container so that live invertebrates have difficulty escaping, and consider sinking it into the substrate so that frogs or toads can easily notice food when it's available. Another good method is to feed by hand or with forceps. This way you can monitor exactly how much food a frog is eating. Both dish-feeding and hand-feeding reduce the chance of having a frog or toad ingest substrate.

## Meeting Nutritional Requirements

### Vitamin and Mineral Supplements

Wild anurans consume a huge variety of foods, but in captivity often we rely on just one or two different types as a staple diet. To help compensate for this, vitamin and mineral

Fruit fly (left) and red flour beetle (right) cultures are available online from feeder insect companies. They make excellent food for tiny frogs.

supplements should be used. These are available at pet stores and come in a powdered form that can be "dusted" onto prey. To do this, place crickets, roaches, or worms into a small container or plastic bag, sprinkle in supplement, and then shake the food until it's lightly coated.

Choose supplements carefully. Unlike human-grade vitamins, there is no regulation of those available for pet amphibians. Take time choosing a reputable one. Check for an expiration date on the container and also ensure that the supplement contains vitamin A. Depending on the supplements, you may need both one that is composed mainly of calcium carbonate and another that is a multivitamin powder. These can then be used alternately or mixed together immediately prior to use.

Growing frogs should have a supplement lightly coated on food at most feedings, while adults may only require supplements at every other meal. It's impossible to know exactly how much supplement is ingested with each feeder or the exact nutritional content of the food prior to being eaten, so quite a bit of guesswork factors into using vitamin and mineral supplements.

## Check the Date

**Vitamin and mineral supplements degrade in quality once they are exposed to air. Keep supplements fresh by replacing them every six months. Write the date on the cover as a reminder of when they must be discarded.**

## Gut Loading

In addition to vitamin and mineral supplements, the nutritional quality of feeders can be increased by "gut loading" them. This means feeding prey foods specifically to enhance or restore the prey's nutritional content.

Crickets, roaches, and worms should all be gut loaded prior to use. Feed a variety of fresh fruits and vegetables for at least two days before they are fed to amphibians. Avoid feeding spinach, beet greens, cabbage, kale, or broccoli. These items may lead to thyroid problems or contain oxalates that inhibit an amphibian's ability to metabolize calcium. Commercially available gut-loading diets designed to enhance the calcium content of feeders are also available, but these must be the only food offered to prey or they usually will be ignored.

*Dyscophus guineti*

# Chapter 4

# Breeding Frogs and Toads in Captivity

**K**eepers can observe many interesting behaviors by breeding amphibians in captivity. Certain frogs exhibit parental care, with the female feeding infertile eggs to a small number of tadpoles until they grow into frogs. Many others produce enormous numbers of young. Some frogs and toads that grow no larger than a human fist can turn out tens of thousands of eggs in one clutch. Males may engage in combat, wrestling each other over prime breeding locations. Those of less aggressive species do not fight, but they still put on a show with their call, singing to attract mates and defend territory.

While some species, such as the African clawed frog and oriental fire-bellied toad, are easy to breed and are produced regularly in captivity, many more are seldom bred. In fact, most frogs and toads have never been bred in captivity. Some may be quite challenging or nearly impossible to breed at home and are best left for experienced hobbyists or zoological institutions, so you should use care in choosing a species to work with. Others can be exceptionally prolific, and the number of offspring may be overwhelming for a first-time frog breeder. Resulting froglets should be sold or traded to hobbyists and herp dealers.

## Sexing

There are several ways frogs can be sexed. It's easiest to do when there are multiple frogs together that can be examined at the same time. Not all species can be sexed in the same way, and even in those that follow the guidelines below there may be differences in individual animals that make determining the sex difficult.

### Calling

Perhaps the easiest way to sex frogs and toads is to listen. Males of most species are vocal and call when exposed to the right conditions. The purpose of an advertisement call is twofold. It attracts females of the same species, and at the same time defends important breeding spots from other males. If you have a group of frogs and are unsure which individuals are calling, examine their throats, which are often dark or baggy-looking following particularly vocal nights.

Just because a frog makes noise does not make it male, however. Females of some species are also vocal, producing calls in response to males or other stimulation. Additionally, frogs of both sexes have distress calls. These notes are usually shorter or squeakier than the typical male advertisement call and occur when an individual is handled, disturbed, or harassed.

### Step One

The first step to breeding is ensuring that your frogs and toads are in good condition. Breeding can be stressful for them, so stressful in fact that it can cause harm or death to weak individuals.

### Nuptial Pads

When in breeding condition, many male frogs develop nuptial pads. These are rough, darkened areas on the forelimbs; they help males hold onto females while in amplexus (the mating embrace). In some species nuptial pads are barely noticeable, being light brown and found on just a single digit; in other anurans they

When male frogs have been calling, their throats often take on a dark coloration, shown here on the western green toad with a female for comparison.

are unmistakable black pads covering much of the foot or lower arm. If you see nuptial pads, the frog is unquestionably male.

## Size and Body Structure

In many frogs females are larger than males. This can be dramatic in some species or quite subtle in others. Males may also have a more streamlined appearance to their body, though this is easy to see only when examining a group of frogs containing both sexes and does not hold true for all species. Other differences in body structure, such as bigger, more muscular arms or simply color, can be used to sex some species. These differences are best used in addition to a more definite sign, such as the presence of nuptial pads or a darkened throat that suggests a male has been calling.

## Seasons and Conditioning

With their strong dependence on water, most frogs and toads are seasonal breeders. For tropical species, wet conditions may persist more than half the year, and breeding is opportunistic as water is available. With frogs or toads from temperate and drier regions, the contrast between seasons can be more dramatic, and breeding may occur during only several rainy weeks of the year.

To breed frogs and toads in captivity, temperature, humidity, water availability, and photoperiod must be manipulated. Sometimes all it takes to spark breeding behavior is a natural increase in temperature and humidity in the room anurans are kept in. Water changes in semi-aquatic and aquatic setups may also fool frogs into thinking that rains have arrived. More often lengthy periods of dry, cool conditions are needed to prep the animals for the breeding season, which is then replicated with dramatic increases in moisture and food

# Maturity

**Most frogs mature within one or two years and only at this point can be sexed and bred. Males of some species begin to call when only a few months old and can sometimes be picked out of a group at this early age. Successful breeding, however, is rare with frogs under a year in age, so wait until the second year for breeding most species.**

availability. This may require a separate breeding enclosure called a rain chamber.

Recreating a dry season or winter can be challenging. In temperate regions, emphasize the temperature changes that naturally occur in the house by moving frogs and toads to a cool location for winter. The temperature should remain constant and not drafty. A basement, cool porch, or garage is a good choice, but check the temperature first to be certain it does not get too cold, especially at night. At cool temperatures, the metabolism of amphibians slows and they require less food. Obesity may result if frogs and toads are fed heavily while being cycled through cool conditions.

Less dramatic winter months can be created by simply shutting off the heat source to a cage and reducing the frequency with which it is misted. This works well for tropical species that do not experience particularly cool conditions in nature. In fact, tropical species exposed to cool conditions may perish, and it is instead the moisture and humidity in the cage that should be changed.

Photoperiod can be adjusted during a dry or cool period as well, with lights being cut back from a normal 12-hour cycle down to around eight to ten hours a day.

The length of a simulated winter or dry season is species dependent. For some, several dry weeks are all that is needed. Others require a three-month rest or even aestivation, during which the prospective breeders burrow into the substrate and require little maintenance. Carefully monitor both the environment and health of frogs and toads exposed to these harsh conditions.

Following a cool dry period, frogs and toads must be convinced the breeding season has arrived. Move the enclosure back to a warm room in the house, turn heating devices on, increase the moisture content of the substrate, and mist the enclosure frequently. These changes should occur over a week so as not to cause too much stress. As their metabolism increases with the increased temperature, frequent feedings are needed. Use a variety of food items and feed heavily to bulk up females so that they produce eggs. Without enough food, properly conditioned males may still call and amplex females, but the girls won't have enough nutrients in them to make eggs.

## Rain Chambers

While some species readily breed in their permanent enclosure, many others require separate housing that is equipped with a rain bar to simulate heavy rains experienced during the breeding season; a housing unit thus equipped is called a rain chamber. A rain bar in its most basic form is a segment of capped-off PVC plastic pipe or flexible tubing that has numerous holes drilled into it. This is then suspended at the top of a waterproof enclosure and connected to a small pump that circulates water up to the rain bar, where it streams out through the holes, simulating a rainstorm. The pump may be located in the bottom of the enclosure in shallow water, or positioned in an external sump if the rain chamber is fitted with a drain. If water rushes out through the holes rather than drips down like rain drops, adjust the pump or drill more holes to relieve pressure.

It's recommended to set the pump on an electrical timer so that it turns off for a period of time each day. If constantly left running, frogs and toads are unable to escape wet conditions and can develop health problems. For some species, the pump may only need to be on for several hours each night; for others it is best if it rains throughout the entire night, stopping during the day when breeding activity normally decreases.

Male frogs call to attract females, and each species has a specific call. The vocal sac amplifies the call, allowing the sound to carry farther.

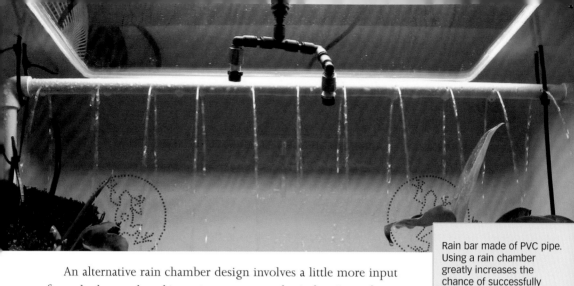

Rain bar made of PVC pipe. Using a rain chamber greatly increases the chance of successfully breeding most frog species.

An alternative rain chamber design involves a little more input from the keeper, but skips using a pump and rain bar. Instead, numerous small holes are drilled into the bottom of a large plastic bucket or container. Set this on top of an enclosure that has a drain built into the bottom, and fill the bucket or container with amphibian-safe water several times each day so that it rains down into the cage. This is a simple design for attempting to breed species in small enclosures and is not practical for breeding larger frogs and toads.

Rain chambers must be built with a particular species in mind. For small terrestrial frogs and toads that migrate to aquatic breeding sites, a standard 20-gallon (76 L) aquarium filled with enough water to submerge a small pump may be adequate. Large tree frogs, on the other hand, should be housed in vertically-oriented rain chambers. A plastic garbage can or special arboreal herp enclosure outfitted with several broad-leafed plants and some floating vegetation in the water below is ideal. Bare-bottom aquarium tanks facilitate quick water changes and high levels of cleanliness. Cork bark, driftwood, and plants should be scattered about the water to help prevent drowning of both frogs and feeder insects. Water temperature plays an important role in the breeding of many amphibians, so it may be advantageous to heat water in rain chambers with a submersible aquarium heater.

## Breeding with Hormones

Some of the most popular pet frogs, such as African clawed frogs and horned frogs, are most often bred with injectable hormones. This can be rough on breeders, so it is usually better to breed frogs and toads the natural way by re-creating seasonal cycles.

Well-conditioned anurans may breed within a day of being placed in the rain chamber, though sometimes it takes a couple weeks before breeding occurs. Watch for breeding behavior from the start. If males are not calling after several days or females do not look swollen with eggs, it's too early and the frogs should be returned to normal housing. They can then be moved back to the rain chamber after a couple of weeks, in the meantime being fed heavily, misted frequently, and monitored for signs of breeding. Some people suggest moving males to the rain chamber several days before females, as the competition between them may help promote breeding success.

Some frogs do not take well to being moved back and forth between their enclosure and a rain chamber. For sensitive species, consider incorporating a rain bar into their normal housing from the start, and plan so that the cage can be rearranged and easily transformed into a rain chamber when needed.

# Eggs

Frogs and toads deposit their eggs in a variety of places. Many lay eggs in large floating mats on the water's surface or in strings attached to aquatic vegetation. Others deposit eggs on objects near the shoreline or in rock crevices overhanging water. Some tree frogs place eggs on leaves that hang above temporary water bodies, while semi-aquatic frogs regularly drape eggs among floating plants.

In order to breed amphibians in captivity, appropriate egg deposition sites must be provided. Useful aquatic plant species include hornwort (*Ceratophyllum* spp.) and anacharis (*Egeria densa*), along with floating and emergent vegetation like parrot's feather (*Myriophyllum aquaticum*) and giant salvinia (*Salvinia molesta*). Clippings of pothos (*Scindapus aureus*) draped through a section of water or in the bottom of the rain chamber also work well as egg deposition sites.

## The Right Time of Year

Numerous breeders have observed their frogs displaying breeding behavior immediately before thunderstorms or during particularly rainy times of the year. It is thought this may be related to natural changes in barometric pressure resulting from approaching storms that amphibians can sense. Consider timing the move to the rain chamber with the onset of spring or a particularly rainy week so that natural fluctuations in pressure coincide with the rainy season created in captivity.

If caves or crevices are needed, try partially submerged flower pots, which are more easily examined for eggs than complex rock structures. For species that deposit eggs next to water, clumps of moist sphagnum moss can be placed at the water's edge under a piece of bark. Broad-leafed plants like Chinese evergreen (*Aglaonema* spp.) and large *Philodendron* species are well suited for tree frogs that deposit eggs on leaves.

Rain chamber made from an aquarium. The emergent plants serve as egg deposition sites—many arboreal frogs lay eggs on leaves overhanging water.

Eggs can be either left to develop where they are laid or carefully moved to a separate aquarium. Fertile eggs do not appear blurry, misshapen, or fuzzy. Development can usually be seen in one or two days' time. Tadpoles may hatch in as little as 18 hours or may take several weeks. This is largely species dependent, though temperature also plays a role. Warmer temperatures speed up the rate of development.

# Tadpoles

Once tadpoles wriggle free from the eggs they remain motionless, moving only if disturbed. Do not feed tadpoles at this early stage of life and keep filtration turned off. As tadpoles use up the remaining nutrients from their yolk sacs over the following week, they begin to move around in search of food. At this point start feeding, performing water changes, and filtering water.

## Housing Tadpoles

There are many approaches to housing tadpoles. Individual cups or small plastic aquaria can be used. Complete water changes must be performed regularly, even daily, if tadpoles are grown in the small volume of water provided by a cup or small plastic aquarium. For raising larger numbers of tadpoles, standard aquaria or plastic storage containers work well. These are best outfitted with sponge filters and aquatic plants, both of which help maintain good water quality. Maintenance for small, simple aquaria involves performing regular partial water changes.

Hundreds or thousands of tadpoles require substantially larger volumes of water. Consider looking into stock tanks or plastic swimming pools for housing. These are more affordable than comparably sized aquaria. Canister filters can be used to help maintain water quality in these large setups.

The same principles involved in maintaining water quality for aquatic frogs or in an aquarium for tropical fish apply to aquaria housing tadpoles. Use as large a volume of water as possible to avoid fluctuations in water quality. Plants not only provide cover for tadpoles but also aid in maintaining a healthy environment for them. Keep up with frequent partial water changes, during which it is important to siphon excess food and waste from the bottom of the tank. Also, remember to use an aquarium water conditioner to remove chlorine and chloramines if tap water is used.

## One Bad Apple...

Remove infertile eggs from a clutch to prevent spoiling the others. A turkey baster can be used to suck up bad eggs laid in water. Razorblades are another useful tool, and can be used to cut out infertile eggs from a clutch laid on land or the side of a cage.

## Feeding Tadpoles

Frog larvae are as diverse as their adult counterparts, and the keeper should adapt the care regimen to suit the species being raised. Feeding styles are varied. Many tadpoles are general scavengers. These types are easy to feed with tropical fish flakes, sinking bottom-feeder pellets, and other fish foods. Other species are predators and should be provided with a carnivorous diet of bloodworms, shrimp pellets, beef heart, and other meaty food items. Some tadpoles are surface feeders and require finely ground floating foods. Many others heavily filter feed and are best raised in aquaria that have been inoculated with infusorians (tiny planktonic organisms).

The use of live or dried algae and algae-based fish foods is recommended for herbivorous tadpoles.

Red-eyed tree frogs in amplexus with their eggs. In some species, including many of the tree frogs, a pair may stay in amplexus for several days.

A simple setup for housing tadpoles using plastic food storage containers. Lights encourage the growth of plants and algae.

Strong lighting helps promote algae growth, which many species enjoy grazing on. Lighting should be placed on a 12-hour photoperiod. Both spirulina and chlorella algae are available in powdered form from health food stores and are widely used by frog breeders. Mix these foods in with ground fish foods to form a staple tadpole diet. Herbivores will voraciously eat dark lettuces and other greens that have been lightly boiled.

## Metamorphosis

Most tadpoles take between one and four months to complete metamorphosis, but there are exceptions. American bullfrogs (*Rana catesbeiana*) may take three years to develop limbs and leave the water, while Budgett's frogs (*Lepidobatrachus laevis*) can complete metamorphosis in as little as 12 days if their water is warm. Temperature, food availability, water quality, and the density at which tadpoles are kept all affect the length of the larval stage.

Once front arms develop, the little tailed frogs require access to land. Terrestrial species easily drown at this point, so monitor them carefully during the later stages of metamorphosis. A floating piece of cork bark, driftwood, or other object should be provided for tadpoles to climb onto. As they are noticed on land, they can be moved to a separate enclosure with shallow water (depending on species, only ½ inch [1.3 cm] or less may be needed) where they are able to fully absorb their tails without the risk of drowning.

It is common to experience high mortality when raising tadpoles, especially during the first few weeks tadpoles are alive and the last while completing metamorphosis. Expect weaker individuals to be out-competed for food and some tadpoles to simply not survive. For the maximum yield, house tadpoles in large volumes of water at low population densities.

## Caring for Young Frogs

Housing young frogs individually or in small groups is best. Plastic storage containers or deli cups work well, especially for species that leave the water at a small size. Alternatively, standard aquariums can be used, but they should not be too large or young frogs may have trouble locating food.

Keep the cage setup simple, with a layer of moist paper towels or sphagnum moss, a water dish, and limited hide spots. Small frogs are prone to desiccation, so make sure the substrate stays moist. As young frogs put on size they can be transferred to larger enclosures.

For the first few days following metamorphosis frogs and toads live off the nutrients gained by absorbing their tails. Following this period they need live food. Small crickets and flightless fruit flies work well for most young frogs, but springtails may be required for some species that need tiny foods. Feed young frogs frequently, lightly coating food items in a calcium or multivitamin supplement at every feeding to ensure that nutritional requirements are met.

## Big Baby Frogs

Tadpoles kept at cooler temperatures take longer to complete metamorphosis but may leave the water at a large size. Consider keeping tadpoles on the cool side of their preferred temperature range to produce big, healthy froglets.

After one to three months the offspring are old enough to be sold to pet stores or dealers or given to other hobbyists. Never release frogs that were bred or raised in captivity, even if they are native to the area where you live. There is a high risk of introducing foreign pathogens to wild amphibian populations through the release of captive-raised frogs.

In some terrestrial frog species (*Mantella aurantiaca* on left and *M. milotympanum* on right), eggs are laid on land and the tadpoles wriggle their way into the water. Here the eggs are set up in moist Java moss over shallow water, so the tadpoles can access the water. When the tadpoles develop their limbs, water depth is reduced and Java moss that rises above the water's surface prevents them from drowning.

*Osteopilus septentrionalis*

# Chapter 5

# Health Care

**W**hen properly cared for many frogs and toads live more than ten years in captivity. Reports of African clawed frogs, White's tree frogs, and horned frogs living upwards of 15 years are not uncommon. To help your frog or toad live its full potential life, it's important to be aware of common health problems that affect amphibians so that you are prepared in case they develop.

## Avoiding Health Problems

Many health problems mentioned in this chapter can be avoided by ensuring that the nutritional requirements of captive frogs and toads are met. Feeding a varied diet that is supplemented appropriately with calcium and vitamins helps ensure a long life. It's also important to pay attention to the environment frogs and toads are housed in. Cleanliness and water quality also must never be overlooked.

Snout abrasions are one of the most common health problems seen in frogs and toads. A Solomon Islands leaf frog with a severely abraded nose is shown here.

### Stress

Stress suppresses an amphibian's immune system, making it susceptible to disease. Fluctuating or inappropriate temperature and humidity levels, the wrong photoperiod, excess live food, a lack of hiding spots, over-aggressive cage mates, and handling are all common causes of stress in captive frogs and toads.

## Veterinarians

It can be difficult to find a local veterinarian who is experienced with amphibians, but doing so is a key to the long-term care of captive frogs and toads. Veterinarians can run tests and prescribe medications that amphibian keepers and pet stores are unable to provide. They also are a superb source of information. If you are not able to find a vet who knows amphibians well, the average furry-animal veterinarian may still be able to help by consulting exotic animal vets.

## Common Diseases and Disorders

### Abrasions, Wounds, and Trauma

Scrapes and abrasions can result from aggressive cage mates, cage items, or bites from live food. Rostral injuries—abrasions of the tip of the snout—from a frog or toad continually trying to escape through the clear sides of an enclosure are also common. Small wounds heal by themselves given time, but if a wound does not appear to be getting better or increases in size after two days it requires treatment.

A triple antibiotic ointment that does not contain pain relievers can be applied to small wounds once a day to help prevent infection. Alternatively, a saline solution (20 grams of sea salt to 1 liter of water) has also been recommended as treatment and should be applied to abrasions with a sterile cotton swab daily, allowed to sit for 10-15 minutes, and then rinsed off with fresh water. Small wounds should heal in about one week. More traumatic wounds and injuries require surgery or amputation, which must be performed by a veterinarian.

## Bacterial Infections

Bacterial infections commonly result when a frog is stressed, kept in unsanitary conditions, or is suffering from another health problem. Symptoms include lethargy, bloating, skin discoloration, lesions, clouded eyes, paralysis, and muscle spasms. Unfortunately, these symptoms often show themselves only once the infection has significantly progressed, making diagnosis in time for treatment difficult. Veterinarians can prescribe broad-spectrum antibiotics to treat bacterial infections, which are either given orally or dropped onto the back, or in which the affected frog or toad is soaked.

"Red leg disease" is a symptom of a bacterial infection heavily discussed in hobbyist literature. With certain types of infections, the underside of the legs appears red from ruptured capillaries. This symptom is frequently observed in addition to others, such as muscle spasms or uncoordinated movements. "Red leg" is often related to fluctuating temperatures, stress, or unsanitary conditions. Treatment involves daily baths in an antibiotic solution prescribed by a veterinarian. Skin can become red for reasons other than a bacterial infection, so it's important to receive a diagnosis from a trained professional before administering medication.

Bacterial infections are difficult to catch in time for treatment, so it's critical that you do not create favorable conditions for them. Dramatic temperature swings, over-stocking, frequent handling, and a

## Nose Rub

Nervous species housed in enclosures that are too small may injure their snouts trying to escape. Minor abrasions may heal on their own if the injured amphibian is moved to a safer enclosure. Poster board taped to the outside of an aquarium prevents nervous species from trying to jump out. It's also helpful is to move jumpy individuals to a room where there is little activity outside the cage so that they feel secure.

dirty cage or water bowl all increase the chance a frog or toad will come down with a bacterial disease.

## Fungal Infections

Fungal infections take many forms. Most often they are seen as small localized discolorations on the skin, often around a lesion or sore. In tadpoles and aquatic frogs, fungal infections that look like stringy gray film or cotton-like fuzz can develop. Like bacterial infections, fungal infections are often secondary to a more severe health problem or can be triggered

This White's tree frog may be suffering from some type of bacterial infection; it's groin is red and inflamed.

by stressful conditions. Treatment depends on the type of infection, which should be determined by a veterinarian. Some hobbyists soak affected frogs in solutions made with fungicidal fish medication, but the success of this treatment is limited.

**Chytridiomycosis** One particular type of fungal infection has proven especially deadly to amphibians and has caused great concern among frog keepers. Chytridiomycosis is a disease caused by the chytrid fungus *Batrachochytrium dendrobatidis* (Bd for short), which is responsible for numerous wild amphibian population declines and extinctions. Bd infections also have caused severe problems for captive frogs and toads, both at zoos and in private collections.

Captive amphibians can get Bd from coming into contact with other infected individuals, husbandry equipment that is shared between cages with infected individuals, and from soil or other moist organic substances that contain infectious spores. Just as concerning as the number of ways captive amphibians can come down with a Bd infection is the fact that they can be infected and not show symptoms for substantial periods of time, infecting others and then dying almost overnight months later after a drop in temperature or stressful situation.

Symptoms that a frog is suffering from chytridiomycosis include excessive shedding or difficulty shedding, constant soaking in the water dish, lethargic behavior, lack of appetite, and a somewhat hunched over or "tucked in" appearance. Bd grows best between a temperature of

59°F (15°C) and 73°F (22.8°C), so often these symptoms do not show when amphibians are kept warm.

Use a careful quarantine procedure when obtaining new frogs or toads; that will help to reduce the chances of dealing with Bd in an amphibian collection. Also, avoid using wood, moss, leaves, and other natural cage décor collected outside unless they are allowed to thoroughly dry or are sterilized with heat.

Treatment of Bd involves soaking infected frogs in a solution of itraconizole, which must be obtained from a veterinarian. This is done daily for one week, during which time all cage items, husbandry equipment, and enclosures must be discarded or sterilized. Some amphibian breeders have used Terbinafine hydrochloride for treatment, which is sold over the counter in many places as an anti-fungal foot spray. This spray is greatly diluted in water (1:200), in which the frogs are soaked for five to ten minutes daily for ten days. Heat is also an effective way to kill the fungus and can be used to sterilize contaminated equipment, with exposure to temperatures above 100°F (37.8°C) for at least four hours doing the job.

## Parasites

Captive amphibians harbor an assortment of microscopic organisms within them, including parasites. Whether or not they are a problem depends on the type of parasite, but also the condition of the frog. Stressed individuals with a suppressed immune system are most likely to suffer from a parasite infection.

Lethargy and weight loss are two common symptoms that are seen when internal parasites reach elevated levels, and if either of these symptoms is noticed, consider bringing the affected frog or toad to a veterinarian for examination. The vet may also request a fecal sample to test for gastrointestinal parasites. Strange growths or spotting can also be a sign of a parasite problem. Treatment varies greatly depending on the type of parasite, but most often involves either an oral medication or medicated bath. The affected anuran's enclosure must be sterilized regularly during the

# Bloat

**There are several reasons an amphibian may become bloated. Often bloating is related to a bacterial infection; other times it is caused by kidney failure resulting from heat stress or poisoning. Gastrointestinal blockages and impaction can also cause an amphibian to appear bloated. Quarantine the affected individual away from other amphibians and seek advice from a veterinarian if a frog or toad swells in size.**

treatment so that the frog or toad is not re-infected.

## Poisoning

With their permeable skin, anurans are quite susceptible to chemical contaminants in their environment. Residue from a cleaning agent used on their enclosure, household cleaners sprayed near the cage, or handling a frog with dirty or dry hands can all result in a poisoned pet. Frogs may also poison themselves if housed at high densities or in unsanitary conditions where waste is allowed to accumulate. Symptoms may include unusually active or agitated behavior and paralysis. Prevention is the key to these problems, so take care when cleaning the house, and always give the enclosure an extra rinse after cleaning it.

Although external parasites are not as common in anurans as in other herps, they do occur. Note the ticks attached to the throat of this southern toad.

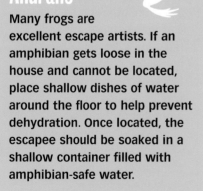

## Escaped Anurans

**Many frogs are excellent escape artists. If an amphibian gets loose in the house and cannot be located, place shallow dishes of water around the floor to help prevent dehydration. Once located, the escapee should be soaked in a shallow container filled with amphibian-safe water.**

## Metabolic Bone Disease

Metabolic bone disease (MBD) is a term used to describe a number of conditions related to an imbalance in the levels of calcium, vitamin $D_3$, and phosphorus in a captive amphibian's diet. Excess vitamin A may also inhibit the ability of frogs to process vitamin D, contributing to MBD. Symptoms include skeletal deformities, causing a frog or toad to look misshapen, especially around the jaws or limbs. Lethargy, tremors, and difficulty in moving may accompany a slightly deformed appearance.

MBD can be avoided by feeding frogs a balanced diet. Calcium, vitamin $D_3$, and phosphorus are not found in the appropriate balanced levels within prey. To offset this, you must use powdered supplements on food items before they are fed to amphibians. Vitamin $D_3$ is used by amphibians to process calcium, so make sure that the calcium supplement used contains $D_3$. Also, because phosphorus inhibits calcium intake, the calcium supplement should have at least a 2:1 ratio of calcium to phosphorus.

## Hypovitaminosis A

Vitamin A plays an important role in the health of frogs, allowing them to feed normally and likely helping produce the important mucus that keeps their skin slimy. When their diet is deficient in vitamin A, symptoms of hypovitaminosis A start to show.

"Short tongue syndrome," in which a frog or toad attempts to feed but has difficulty pulling prey into its mouth because its tongue lacks the sticky mucus needed to do so, is a sign of a vitamin A deficiency. Swollen eyes, lesions below the eyes, or the development of skin infections may also indicate an amphibian is suffering from hypovitaminosis A. Be certain that vitamin supplements contain vitamin A and that they are less than six months old to help prevent hypovitaminosis A.

## Obesity

One of the most enjoyable parts of keeping frogs is feeding them, but when fed too often or when calorie-dense foods (such as rodents or fish) are overused, obesity can result. This is a common health problem that has serious consequences. You can tell an obese frog from one with a healthy weight by the rolls of fat that show around the arms, eyes, or chin. Avoid feeding foods such as wax worms, rodents, or fish to obese amphibians, and cut back on their feeding schedule. Earthworms and night crawlers are particularly healthy foods to use, so try substituting them for crickets if you have a fat frog.

The environment a frog or toad is maintained in plays a role in its metabolism. If kept on the cool side of its preferred temperature range, a frog or toad will not require much food. During cool months of the year the feeding schedule may need to be adjusted to prevent frogs and toads from becoming obese.

## Stale Supplements

An often overlooked aspect of frog and toad care that contributes to nutritional disorders is the age of nutritional supplements. Vitamins in supplements degrade once exposed to air, especially when stored in humid or warm locations. Replace supplements at least once every six months to avoid nutritional disorders.

Obesity is a common problem in large frogs that are fed too many rodents, such as ornate horned frogs.

## Corneal Lipidosis

While there are many reasons why a frog's eyes may appear clouded or white, corneal lipidosis is one of the more common disorders that cause this condition. Cholesterol deposits form on various organs in the body in obese amphibians, including the eye. They may first be noticed as small white markings that increase in size over time. This results in reduced vision or blindness, and because most frogs and toads use their eyes to locate food, it can cause serious problems.

Have a veterinarian examine amphibians if white spots start developing on their eyes. Treatment involves switching to a low-fat diet and providing access to particularly warm areas in the enclosure to increase the metabolism of the affected frog or toad. Amphibians suffering from corneal lipidosis have been known to survive for years following diagnosis, but other problems that result from obesity often take their toll before they survive that long.

## Impaction

Many frogs and toads feed aggressively, lunging at food items with an open mouth. Sometimes an overzealous anuran also swallows some of the substrate it is kept on along with a meal. If the animal is unable to pass the substrate, an impaction can result. Prevention is the key, otherwise surgery is required, which is expensive and not always possible depending on the species, what it has swallowed, and the veterinarians you have access to. Some substrates such as pea gravel are notorious for causing impactions. Consider feeding frogs and toads by hand or in a dish if using a risky substrate. Symptoms of an impaction include lack of appetite and abdominal swelling.

## Prolapses

A prolapse occurs when an organ slips out of place. Rectal and cloacal prolapses are not uncommon; they look as though pink internal tissue is hanging out of the vent. Causes of a prolapse are often related to diet but may also be the result of a parasite infection or gastrointestinal blockage. Feeding too heavily can also contribute to a prolapse. Sometimes the tissue that has fallen out of place fixes itself and is absorbed back into the body, but if nothing changes after two days, consult a veterinarian. Dabbing the protruding tissue with sugar water affects osmotic regulation, reduces swelling, and may aid the situation.

## Yawning Frogs

When frogs and toads shed their skin, they may appear as though they are yawning. This occurs as they eat the extras and stretch to pull skin off the body. "Yawning" is completely normal, and unless they shed excessively or have difficulty doing so, there is no reason to be alarmed.

Tomato frog eating its shed skin.

*Bombina orientalis*

# Chapter 6

# Fire-Bellied Toads

**W**ith their flashy coloration and hardy nature, fire-bellied toads make some of the best captive amphibians there are. The Oriental fire-bellied toad is most commonly encountered, but others, such as the yellow-bellied toad also are offered for sale from time to time. They are resilient creatures, tolerating a wide range of captive conditions, and make a great first pet amphibian.

# Description of Species

Depending on which taxonomist one follows, there are five to eight species in *Bombina*. Only care for the four available in the pet trade will be covered in this chapter, although care for the others is likely quite similar.

## Oriental Fire-Bellied Toad

Painted in a contrasting set of colors, the Oriental fire-bellied toad (*Bombina orientalis*) is the *Bombina* most often encountered in pet stores. Like the other fire-bellies, this toad's scarlet red ventral side warns predators that it is poisonous. When sitting normally, however, the belly is concealed and the toad blends into its surroundings with a dorsal side that varies from bright green to brown or even black. Dark markings coat the body, giving *B. orientalis* an exotic look. Oriental fire-bellied toads grow at most to just over 2.0 inches (5.1 cm) in length.

B. *orientalis* is native to Korea, northeast China, and a small corner of Russia. It lives a largely aquatic life at the water's edge. Wild toads live alongside streams, in rice paddies, and near small ponds. In certain parts of their range they are surprisingly abundant, especially during the spring breeding season when they congregate at breeding sites in large numbers.

## Yellow-Bellied Toad

Smaller in size than the Oriental fire-bellied toad, the yellow-bellied toad (*Bombina variegata*) matures at around 1.6 inches (4.0 cm) in length. Its dorsal side is dirty olive-green, while ventrally it is yellow-orange, patterned in black. The yellow-bellied toad is only occasionally encountered in the North American pet trade—usually as captive-bred stock imported from Europe.

B. *variegata* is native to central and southern Europe, where it can be found in a variety of habitats, from flooded mountain meadows to forest ponds. Breeding most often occurs in temporary water bodies. There are records of the yellow-bellied toad's hybridizing with the European fire-bellied toad in areas where their ranges overlap.

## Toxic Toads

All **Bombina** species have brightly colored bellies that warn predators of their poisonous skin secretions. There is no reason to fear their mildly toxic nature, but to be safe always wash hands after coming in contact with a toad.

## European Fire-Bellied Toad

The European fire-bellied toad (*Bombina bombina*) looks like the yellow-bellied toad, but with a fiery orange-red belly

Dorsal and ventral views of the oriental fire-bellied toad, showing the namesake belly.

and slightly smoother skin. It is only rarely found for sale because they have proven more difficult to breed than other *Bombina* species. Ranging throughout central and eastern Europe, the European fire-bellied toad is often found near stagnant pools of water along river valleys, but it also inhabits marshes and other wetlands.

## Giant Fire-Bellied Toad

As its common name suggests, the giant fire-bellied toad (*Bombina maxima*) is the largest member of the genus, growing to slightly over 2.5 inches (6.5 cm). Dorsally it is a variable shade of brown or gray, covered in large warts. The belly is light orange with big dark blotches. *B. maxima* is native to southern China and neighboring northern Vietnam. On odd occasions this species shows up in the pet trade as a result of successful captive breeding in Europe, but it is still quite rare in collections.

## Captive Care

Fire-bellied toad care is undemanding. Most important is providing a suitable environment with an easily maintained aquatic area. Feeding a varied diet is the key to long-term health. Captive fire-bellied toads will live more than a decade when given proper care.

## Acquisition

Pet stores regularly stock imported Oriental fire-bellied toads. When selecting toads, first examine the conditions they are kept in. While fire-bellies tolerate crowding temporarily, toads housed at high densities may be stressed and in poor condition. A healthy fire-bellied toad should have clear eyes and look alert, not hunched over or lethargic. Select strong individuals that are plump, with a slightly rounded body. Pass up fire-bellied toads that are housed with other species of amphibians, because they may have been exposed to foreign pathogens to which they have no resistance. The best way of ensuring you start with good toads is to find a local breeder through a herpetological society or hobbyist forums on the Internet.

Yellow-bellied toad in the defensive posture known as the unken reflex, which displays the bright warning colors and the feet and belly.

Locating the other *Bombina* species requires a bit more work than just taking a trip to the pet store. They are best found through reptile and amphibian dealers or herp classifieds online.

Fire-bellied toads are most enjoyable to keep in groups. Territorial disputes between males can result in entertaining wrestling matches, while keeping females in the mix provides the opportunity to raise eggs and tadpoles. Four to six toads is a good number to start with.

## Housing

Fire-bellied toads are simple to house. A standard 10-gallon (38-l) aquarium is sufficient space for a trio, while up to six can be housed in a 20-gallon (75.7-l) aquarium. Although they don't appear particularly agile, fire-bellied toads are actually quite talented climbers, so use a secure screen cover to prevent escapes.

*Bombina* are semi-aquatic animals, spending much of their time in shallow water along the shoreline. Housing must therefore include a

The European fire-bellied toad has proven challenging to breed, but it is no more difficult to keep than the more common species.

substantial area of water. The simplest way to accomplish this is to use a substrate of coconut husk fiber or long-fiber sphagnum moss several inches deep. Sink a large water dish into this substrate, allowing easy access to water. Plastic storage containers, pet food bowls, or specialty herp water bowls all work well for this purpose. Add a couple of hide spots, such as driftwood or artificial plants, on top of the substrate. This is especially important if keeping more than one toad.

Another strategy for creating a habitat for fire-bellied toads involves a little more work but is more aesthetically pleasing. Use a piece of cork bark, several large stones, or a tree fern slab to divide the enclosure in half. Fill one side of the divider almost all the way with gravel to form a terrestrial habitat for the toads. Leave the other side with less than 1.0 inch (2.5 cm) of this substrate. Then fill the enclosure with water, up to the top of the land area. Cover the land area with moist sphagnum moss to prevent the toads from accidentally ingesting gravel. Maintenance for this type of semi-aquatic setup involves weekly partial water changes.

Hardy live plants, such as pothos or wandering Jew, can be planted in the land area. Their root systems will eventually hold the gravel in place behind the divider. Amazon frogbit can be grown in the water to form aquatic resting areas for the toads. While the toads do not require any special lighting, any live plants you include will need one or two fluorescent bulbs running the length of the setup. Adding lights will allow the inclusion of live plants and will also enhance the overall appearance of the enclosure.

# The Other Fire-Bellies

*Bombina fortinuptialis:* Known from only a small section of Guanxi Province in southern China, *B. fortinuptialis* is a rare species, with only a handful of individuals having been found since its description in 1978. Some consider it a subspecies of *B. maxima*.

*Bombina lichuanensis:* Little is known about this newly described fire-bellied toad, which is native to marshes in high-altitude forests in Sichuan Province, China.

*Bombina microdeladigitora:* Most now consider *B. microdeladigitora* to be synonymous with *B. maxima*, though in hobbyist literature this fire-bellied toad is sometimes mentioned as a separate species.

*Bombina pachypus:* Restricted to Italy, *B. pachypus* appears much like *B. variegata*. It has suffered severe population declines over the last decade, possibly due to chytridiomycosis. Some consider *B. pachypus* to be a subspecies of *B. variegata*.

## Toads and Newts

It's common to see fire-bellied toads housed with Chinese fire-bellied newts (*Cynops orientalis*), but this is a risky combination. Fire-bellied toads are aggressive feeders and often bite the limbs or tails off newts in an attempt to eat them. Additionally, newts prefer cooler temperatures and deeper water than fire-bellied toads, and the toxins both species produce are capable of causing harm to the other.

## Temperature and Humidity

Ideally, the enclosure should be maintained between 72°F (22.2°C) and 78°F (25.6°C) during the day with a drop in temperature of around 5°F (3°C) each night. Note that for *B. maxima* the temperature must remain cooler, preferably only rising to around 65°F (18.3°C) during the day. In warmer climates room temperature may suffice for keeping fire-belied toads. A low-power light bulb can be added above the land area to bring about an increase in temperature during the day if needed.

Healthy fire-bellies tolerate cool temperatures well, with drops to 50°F (10°C) presenting no problem as long as the change in temperature is gradual. Warm temperatures can result in heat stress, though, so make sure to cool the cage if temperatures rise above 80°F (26.7°C).

Average household humidity levels of 40 to 60 percent are appropriate for fire-bellied toads. Consider misting the enclosure with water several times each week to keep the substrate slightly damp and to bring about the temporary increases in humidity wild toads would experience following rain.

## Diet

A fire-bellied toad diet should be composed of a variety of live invertebrates. Feed adult toads two to six food items every couple of days. Crickets can form the bulk of the diet, but make sure to substitute other food items for crickets every few feedings. Wax worms, small earthworms, and other similarly sized prey work well and can be fed in a shallow feeding dish. Some people also have luck feeding small guppies and ghost shrimp to toads. Coat nonaquatic food items in high-quality calcium and vitamin supplements at every other feeding to ensure that nutritional requirements are met.

## Breeding

Oriental fire-bellied toads and yellow-bellied toads regularly breed in captivity when exposed to seasonal changes in temperature, humidity, and photoperiod. The European fire-bellied toad and giant fire-bellied toad are a bit more difficult to breed in captivity, even when provided with suitable seasonal cycles. Many people report the best breeding success when keeping a large male-heavy group of fire-bellied toads. If breeding is your goal, try to have at least two males for every female in the group.

## Sexing

Fire-bellied toads can be sexed by examining body structure. The front arms of males appear more muscular than those of females, while their overall body size and shape are sometimes smaller and more streamlined. This may differ between individuals, however, and it can be confusing when looking at obese or underweight toads.

A more reliable way to sex fire-bellied toads is to examine the males during the breeding season. Male toads develop dark nuptial pads on the first and second digits when in breeding condition. Males also vocalize to defend territory and attract mates. Their call is soft and rhythmic, with a short repeated note. Only adult toads can be sexed, and they become mature between one and two years of age.

The giant fire-bellied toad is the largest and wartiest species. It occasionally is captive bred in Europe.

## Seasonal Conditioning

To breed fire-bellied toads in captivity, the keeper must expose them to conditions that replicate their breeding season in the wild. Sometimes this may happen unintentionally. A water change following a slight increase in household temperature can be enough to trick toads into thinking it is the breeding season. Most often, though, a cool, dry, artificial winter is needed in order to provide enough contrast in temperature, humidity, and light levels to stimulate captive *Bombina* to spawn.

Start by decreasing the temperature in the enclosure to around 60°F (15.6°C) for *B. orientalis*, slightly cooler for the other species. At the same time, cut back on misting the enclosure and reduce feeding frequency. Fire-bellied toads often burrow under cage items during a cool dry period in order to conserve moisture. Realize that exposing toads to these conditions can be stressful, so only condition healthy individuals that have been in your care for a substantial period of time.

After six to eight weeks of a cool artificial winter, begin to warm toads back up to normal conditions. Mist the enclosure daily to increase humidity levels and feed heavily. Some breeders also suggest increasing light intensity and photoperiod during this time.

Males will soon begin to call if conditions are right. When a female approaches (or sometimes just another male toad), the calling male will amplex her. Females lay between 30 and 150 eggs, most often attached singly or in small clumps to vegetation near the water's edge. It's

**top**: Pair of oriental fire-bellied toads in amplexus. This species normally breeds after several weeks of cool and dry conditions.
**center**: Eggs of the giant fire-bellied toad. The two whitish eggs have gone bad and should be removed from the rest of the clutch.
**bottom**: Three-week old oriental fire-bellied froglets with a ruler to show their tiny size.

recommended to remove eggs to a separate enclosure so that they are not disturbed while developing.

## Tadpole and Froglet Care

If eggs are fertile, tadpoles wriggle free in three to ten days. Maintain them at a temperature between 60°F (15.6°C) and 72°F (22.2°C). During the first week, tadpoles likely will not feed, sitting motionless at the bottom of the aquarium as they absorb their yolk sacs. After this period tadpoles are quite voracious and can be offered fish flakes, bloodworms, *Tubifex*, daphnia, and other foods daily. Perform partial water changes on a regular basis to maintain good water quality.

Once front arms develop, move the little toads to a new enclosure. This should have a large section of shallow water, as well as a land area that is easy to access, such as a floating piece of cork bark. Live foods can be offered once the tail is fully absorbed. Newly morphed fire-bellied toads measure just under 0.8 inches (2.0 cm) and should be fed flightless fruit flies, springtails, or hatchling crickets daily. Use high quality calcium and vitamin supplements to ensure that nutritional requirements are met.

*Fire-Bellied Toads*    75

*Ceratophrys ornata*

# Chapter 7

# Horned Frogs and African Bullfrogs

t is commonplace to see nickel-sized horned frogs and African bullfrogs for sale at pet stores. When given the proper care, these adorable little mouths with eyes quickly turn into ferocious ambush predators. Feeding them is the most enjoyable part of their care, because other than eat, they really don't do much. Care is undemanding, and because both frogs come from somewhat harsh environments in the wild, they tolerate a wide range of conditions in captivity.

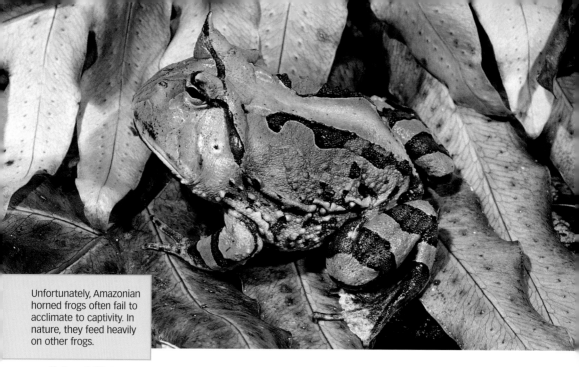

Unfortunately, Amazonian horned frogs often fail to acclimate to captivity. In nature, they feed heavily on other frogs.

## Natural History

The horned frog genus *Ceratophrys* contains eight species, all of which are native to South America. They live a strongly seasonal existence, aestivating in a cocoon of mucus in the ground throughout the dry season. When rain finally comes, horned frogs awaken and begin to feed and breed. Wild horned frogs enjoy a diet of other frogs, lizards, and large invertebrates. Their tadpoles are also highly predatory, feeding mainly on other tadpoles and insect larvae.

Three species of African bullfrogs are found across the Atlantic; they are not closely related to the South American horned frogs, but they live a similarly seasonal life. They inhabit dry savannahs and grasslands. For most of the year, African bullfrogs remain underground to conserve moisture, but when rain arrives, these beastly frogs emerge to put on weight and find a mate. Large congregations of African bullfrogs gather at temporary water pools where breeding takes place.

## Description of Available Species

### Amazonian Horned Frog

Only occasionally available, the Amazonian horned frog (*Ceratophrys cornuta*) exhibits pointed projections above the eyes that make it clear where the name "horned frog" comes from. Their coloration varies from tan to lime green, normally with a pattern of thick darkened stripes extending outwards down the body. Large females can reach 4.7 inches (12.0 cm), while males normally do not grow larger than 2.8 inches (7.2 cm). They range throughout the Amazon basin and have the largest distribution of all *Ceratophrys* species.

Most often wild-caught Amazonian horned frogs that have proven difficult to acclimate to captivity, and especially to feed, have been offered for sale. Sometimes they must be force-fed, and other times they never take to a captive life and waste away. Fortunately, captive-bred juveniles are also occasionally found for sale. They are substantially easier to keep, feeding well on the usual fare of invertebrates and an occasional mouse.

## Chacoan Horned Frog

The Chacoan horned frog (*Ceratophrys cranwelli*) is the most commonly encountered species of *Ceratophrys* in the pet trade. Numerous color morphs are available. Brown and green individuals are most often seen, but the hue of these colors varies, from rusty red to turquoise blue. An albino form is yellow in coloration. *C. cranwelli* is native to the arid Chaco region of South America, where it breeds explosively during the wet season. As adults, females grow to around 4.0 inches (10.2 cm), while males stay closer to 3.0 inches (7.6 cm).

## Ornate Horned Frog

Also called Bell's horned frog, the ornate horned frog (*Ceratophrys ornata*) is a colorful species. Most often their coloration consists of green with varying amounts of russet brown to rust-colored spots. Some may instead have dark green or even red blotching over a lighter background color. Large females can grow to 5 inches (13 cm) in length, but most do not reach this impressive size. Males are smaller, to around 3.5 inches (8.9 cm). The ornate horned frog is native to grasslands in the Pampas region of Argentina, Uruguay, and a small corner of Brazil.

## Fantasy Frogs

Hybrids of *C. cornuta* and *C. cranwelli* are offered for sale under the common name "fantasy frog." Their body

## A Toe Trap

The Venezuelan horned frog (*C. calcarata*) and ornate horned frog (*C. ornata*) have been observed luring food items with their toes. They sit motionless, blending into the forest floor until prey approaches. When food is noticed, they reveal their yellow toes, which are wiggled to attract the prey. Once close enough, the horned frog lunges forward and devours the meal.

structure appears similar to that of C. cornuta, but with shorter fleshy horns over the eyes. Fantasy frogs exhibit a wide range of colors, from orange and green to gray with purple tones. Their care is the same as for other horned frogs, and they are perfect for the keeper who wants a frog that resembles C. cornuta without the associated high price and feeding difficulties.

## Giant African Bullfrog

The giant African bullfrog (Pyxicephalus adspersus) is an impressive amphibian. Males can attain lengths of 10 inches (25 cm), though more commonly they are between 7 and 9 inches (18 and 23 cm). Unusual for frogs and toads, female African bullfrogs are smaller than males, rarely exceeding 5 inches (13 cm). P. adsperus is also called the giant pixie frog. Juvenile coloration is quite attractive, with a neon green stripe cutting through a dark gray-green dorsum. As bullfrogs mature, they end up with a uniformly olive-green back and cream-colored belly, bordered by gold. P. adspersus has a wide range throughout southern Africa, from Tanzania and southern Kenya down through South Africa.

## Dwarf African Bullfrog

Smaller than the giant African bullfrog is Pyxicephalus edulis, the dwarf African bullfrog or dwarf pixie frog. Its overall body structure is similar to that of P. adspersus, though dorsal coloration tends more towards brown or gray than green. Additionally, the yellow found around the flanks and throat may be more prominent, especially in males. Both male and female dwarf African

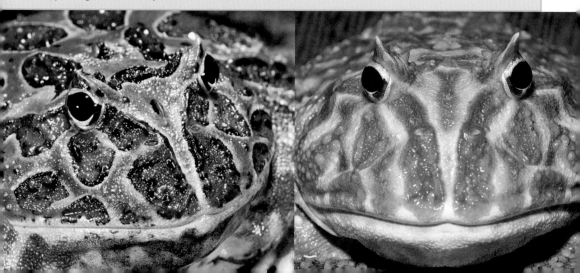

Normal (left) and albino (right) Chacoan horned frogs. Commercial breeders produce large numbers of this species, mostly through the use of reproductive hormones.

# Budgett's Frogs

Budgett's frogs—members of the same subfamily as *Ceratophrys*—can be found for sale as a result of captive breeding at the same facilities that produce Pacmans and African bullfrogs. Two species, *Lepidobatrachus laevis* and the slightly smaller *L. llanensis*, are available. Females of the former grow up to 4.8 inches (12.2 cm), with males maturing closer to 3.3 inches (8.4 cm).  Both are ugly frogs, with grotesque wrinkly gray skin and funny upturned eyes that look constantly surprised.

Traditionally, Budgett's frogs have been kept in aquatic setups, but this has not always been met with success. In the Chaco, wild *Lepidobatrachus* encounter wet conditions during the four-month-long wet season only, aestivating below ground the rest of the year. Keep Budgett's frogs like horned frogs, but with a substantially larger, deeper pool of water. Consider providing seasonal variation in temperature, moisture, and photoperiod so that they are allowed to aestivate several months of the year as well. Budgett's frogs feed well on the usual fare of crickets and worms.

bullfrogs grow close to 4.5 inches (11.7 cm) in length, though males are substantially more heavyset. The distribution of *P. edulis* overlaps that of *P. adspersus*, but it does not extend as far south. The two were considered the same species until the mid 1990's.

## Captive Care

### Acquisition

Ornate and Chacoan horned frogs are widely available from pet stores. Although tiny thumbnail-sized babies are cute, you should select older individuals if available. Frogs near the size of a half-

Fantasy frogs (left) are hybrids of Amazonian horned frogs (right) and Chacoan horned frogs. They greatly resemble the Amazonians but make much hardier pets.

dollar or larger are best. Amazonian horned frogs can be difficult to locate. Wild-caught adults fare poorly in captivity and should be purchased by experienced keepers only. African bullfrogs are less frequently available than ornate and Chacoan horned frogs, but when breeders have success, little pyxie frogs are abundant at reptile shows and pet stores.

Regardless of which species you plan to acquire, examine the animals carefully before making a purchase. Healthy horned frogs and African bullfrogs have good weight and look rotund. Also, look at the conditions the frog is kept in. Avoid purchasing frogs that are housed in dirty conditions. It is common practice to temporarily house juveniles in deli cups lined with paper towels, but this housing can lead to health problems unless high levels of cleanliness are maintained.

## Housing

Horned frogs and African bullfrogs are ambush predators, so they wait for food to come to them and are not especially active. One result is that in captivity they do not require much space.

An adult horned frog can be successfully maintained in a standard 10-gallon (38-l) aquarium. African bullfrogs must be provided with larger housing because they are bigger than horned frogs. Adults require a 20-gallon (75.7-l) aquarium, with monster males doing best when given more room. Use a screen cover to prevent curious children or pets from disturbing the frog in its enclosure and also so that the occasionally active frog does not escape. Horned frogs and African bullfrogs are best housed alone, especially as juveniles, because of their cannibalistic tendencies.

There are several substrate options. Coconut husk fiber is an excellent choice. Sphagnum moss or cypress mulch works fairly well too, though it's best to feed food from forceps if using a substrate that could cause problems if swallowed. Pay attention to the moisture content of the substrate. If it dries, frogs may begin to aestivate, wrapping themselves in a thick layer of skin and mucus to conserve water. In this state they do not feed. Simple substrates can also be used. In particular, many people find foam rubber works well.

Over the substrate consider placing a piece of cork bark or driftwood. This will create microclimates within the enclosure, as well as reducing stress in setups with a simple substrate wherein the frog cannot burrow to hide. Add a water dish large enough for frogs to soak in. The water depth should be about half as high as the frog is tall. Horned frogs and African bullfrogs regularly use their water dish as a toilet, so keep it clean, replacing water daily.

Giant African bullfrogs definitely live up to their common name, with males sometimes reaching 10 inches (25 cm) in length.

## Temperature and Humidity

While horned frogs and African bullfrogs cope with temperature extremes in the wild, in captivity it's best to avoid large fluctuations. Provide a temperature range between 75°F and 84°F (24°C and 29°C). Use a low-power (normally not more than 50 watts) heat lamp directed over part of the cage to achieve this temperature range. At night, the temperature can decrease by 5° to 10°F (3° to 6°C).

Coming from somewhat arid regions, Chacoan and ornate horned frogs, along with African bullfrogs, live well in captivity with average household humidity levels between

# Common Name Game

Collectively, members of the genus *Ceratophrys* are known as horned frogs because of the pointed horn-like projections that are found above the eyes of species like *C. cornuta*. Their gigantic mouths and round bodies are reminiscent of a familiar video game character, and more often than not they are called Pacman frogs in the pet trade.

*Pyxicephalus* species are widely known as African bullfrogs but also are regularly called pyxie or pixie frogs. This name originates from the first half of their scientific name, *Pyxicephalus*. The dwarf African bullfrog, *P. edulis*, is also known as the edible bullfrog because it is used as food in some parts of its range.

35 and 60 percent. You can lightly mist the enclosure with water several times a week to ensure that the substrate does not dry, and to bring about temporary increases in humidity that keep horned frogs alert and feeding. Coming from the Amazon, the Amazonian horned frog prefers higher levels of humidity. Spray the enclosure daily to maintain a tropical environment for them.

## Diet

Ask any horned frog or African bullfrog keeper what their favorite part of care is and they will undoubtedly tell you it is watching their frog eat. These aggressive anurans have a ferocious appetite, and as a result people love to feed them. Unfortunately, the most common errors made when keeping horned frogs and African bullfrogs is feeding inappropriate food items and feeding too much food too often. Obesity and nutritional deficiencies are common, so develop a good feeding schedule for your frog, composed of healthy food items in just the right amount.

Juveniles readily consume crickets, which make a great staple diet. Feed two to four every couple days. Substitute other foods for crickets, such as earthworms or guppies, every few feedings.

As the frogs grow, begin feeding larger food items like night crawlers, minnows, cockroaches, and superworms. Night crawlers in particular are an excellent food for adult frogs. A good feeding schedule consists of one or two night crawlers or large roaches once a week, skipping or delaying a feeding every now and then. Pre-killed mice and rat pups are also accepted as food, although they are not ideal food items. While it's impressive to watch an African bullfrog or horned frog scarf down a pre-killed mouse, feeding rodents frequently leads to nutritional problems. Instead, use rodents sparingly—less than once a month if at all.

Nutritional deficiencies are common in growing young horned frogs and African bullfrogs. Use a calcium supplement that contains vitamin $D_3$ as well as a high-quality multivitamin supplement to help prevent nutritional disorders from developing.

Sometimes horned frogs and African bullfrogs refuse to feed. This is especially common when there are changes in environmental conditions. In temperate climates, the temperature and humidity in the house may decrease when the seasons change, unintentionally tricking frogs into thinking the dry season is approaching. If a frog refuses food, check the temperature and humidity in the enclosure, and if necessary mist frequently and upgrade to a more powerful light bulb. Well-fed adult horned frogs and African bullfrogs can go months without food in captivity, but it's best to keep their metabolism up to par so that they feed regularly.

Dwarf African bullfrogs appear very similar to their giant relatives. The white spot on the tympanum is distinctive of the dwarf.

## Breeding

Both horned frogs and African bullfrogs are regularly bred in captivity. Most captive-bred stock originates from several large breeding facilities that specialize in supplying these frogs to the pet trade. Breeding facilities usually use hormonal injections to produce mass quantities of frogs, but the persistent individual looking to spawn a pair or two through a more natural method of seasonal conditioning will find great rewards.

Be prepared for a bit of work, though, including months of

preparation followed by hundreds of highly cannibalistic tadpoles and froglets to care for. Note that there is no reliable documentation of African bullfrogs being bred in captivity without the use of hormones or large outdoor enclosures, so this is quite the worthwhile challenge to pursue if you have the space and resources.

## Sexing

Male horned frogs can be told apart from females in several ways. Easiest is to look at the size of several adult animals together. Females average slightly larger than males, often by 0.5 inches (1.3 cm) or more. Male horned frogs that have been calling have a slightly darkened, baggy-looking throat. Females do not call. When in breeding condition, males can be told apart from females by the dark nuptial pads that develop on the toes of their front feet. This can be tricky to see in albino Chacoan horned frogs, but is otherwise quite apparent.

Although horned frogs don't have actual teeth, they have a sharp bony ridge on the bottom jaw (seen here on an ornate horned frog) that serves a similar function.

Giant African bullfrogs can also be sexed based on adult size, but it is the male which is larger. They can grow almost twice the size of females. In contrast, both male and female dwarf African bullfrogs remain close in size as adults, though males still appear a bit on the hefty side. The call of a male African bullfrog is a "long, low-pitched whoop," often produced during the day. Females are silent.

## Feeding With Forceps

**Consider feeding with forceps. Not only does this help prevent frogs from ingesting bedding along with prey, it also protects keepers and their fingers from a painful bite.**

## Conditioning

When the rains arrive in their natural habitat, horned frogs and African bullfrogs emerge from a semi-dormant state and begin to feed heavily in preparation for breeding. Temporary pools of water form from rain and serve as breeding sites. This transition from dry, arid conditions to persistent thunderstorms triggers a breeding response. In order to breed horned frogs and African bullfrogs in captivity seasonal changes in temperature, photoperiod, humidity, and water availability must be provided.

Start by preparing frogs for aestivation with a month of heavy feeding, followed by two weeks without food under normal conditions to empty their gut. Then move the frogs to enclosures with at least 4 inches (10.2 cm) of a substrate in which they can burrow. Cool the enclosure to between 55° and 65°F (13° and 18°C) for Chacoan and ornate horned frogs, and several degrees warmer for African bullfrogs and Amazonian horned frogs. Additionally, you must reduce humidity, moisture content of the substrate, and photoperiod. Make sure that the substrate does not completely dry to avoid desiccation. Horned frogs and African bullfrogs will not feed during this time, or do much of anything other than wait for the temperature to warm and water to become available.

After four to eight weeks of these harsh conditions, begin warming frogs back up to the normal temperature range. This should be gradual and occur over the course of a week or so. While increasing the temperature, begin adding water to the substrate to increase the moisture content. Once frogs have emerged from underground and shed their layer of moisture-retentive skin, begin to feed. Under normal conditions, weekly feedings are best for adult frogs, but in order to prepare them for breeding offer food daily.

## The Rain Chamber

To stimulate breeding activity, create a rain chamber that replicates the heavy storms experienced in nature during the rainy season. If attempting to breed African bullfrogs, use as large an enclosure as possible, such as a large

When conditions are too dry for them, horned frogs hide underground and wrap themselves in a water-retaining cocoon of skin and mucus.

A wild male giant African bullfrog calling. Captive African bullfrogs seem to need large outdoor enclosures for successful breeding.

stock tank or cattle watering trough. Keep the water shallow, around 1 inch (2.5 cm) for horned frogs and up to 3 inches (7.6 cm) for African bullfrogs, and heat it to 82°F (27.8°C) with a submersible aquarium heater. Horned frogs in particular are poor swimmers and are prone to drowning if water is too deep.

Plants such as pothos and anacharis should be scattered about the water to provide surfaces for egg deposition. Some people recommend timing a move to the rain chamber with the onset of an especially rainy week. The drop in barometric pressure or other slight changes caused by the arrival of thunderstorms may help trigger a breeding response in captive frogs.

If all goes well, male horned frogs begin calling to attract females. Their call is a repetitive metallic honk; they produce it most often at night. Introduce a female if males are calling, paying close attention to ensure the frogs don't drown or attempt to eat each other. If mating is successful, you will see eggs scattered about the water, especially around vegetation, within a week.

A successful horned frog breeding produces anywhere from 200 to more than 2,000 eggs. African bullfrogs may produce more than 10,000 eggs. If no eggs are found after one week in the rain chamber, move frogs back to their normal housing, feed heavily for one more week, and then try again. Tadpoles start to hatch from eggs within one day of being laid and begin feeding soon after.

## Tadpole and Froglet Care

Both horned frog and African bullfrog tadpoles are vicious predators. Several large aquariums are needed, allowing you to sort the tadpoles by size to reduce cannibalism as they grow. No matter how hard you try, it is likely many tadpoles will be lost to the hunger of their siblings. Commercial breeders have found live blackworms to work well as a food source. Frozen fish foods, such as bloodworms and beef heart, as well as chopped earthworms, can also be used as tadpole food. Feed heavily to reduce fin-nipping, leg-biting, and predation.

At a temperature of 81°F (27.2°C), the first horned frog tadpoles begin to leave the water in as little as three weeks. It takes a bit longer before African bullfrog tadpoles start to metamorphose. Provide floating pieces of cork bark, Styrofoam, and/or vegetation onto which morphing frogs can crawl out of the water. Once they are on land, move the tailed froglets to a separate container to avoid drowning.

## Fighting Frogs

Male African bullfrogs (*P. adspersus*) regularly engage in combat at breeding sites in the wild. Wrestling matches can be quite fierce, sometimes resulting in death. While competition can help simulate breeding, you should not let your frogs actually engage in combat.

Individual containers are needed to house each juvenile horned frog or African bullfrog so that they do not eat one another. Deli cups, plastic storage containers, or aquariums that are partitioned into sections are all good options. Feed young frogs crickets, guppies, and worms, supplemented with appropriate vitamin and minerals daily, keeping them around 81°F (27.2°C) so that their metabolism is high and they put on size quickly. After three weeks they are usually large enough to sell.

Ornate horned frog tadpole with hind legs. Horned frog and African bullfrog tadpoles are cannibalistic, so keep them well fed or in individual containers.

*Litoria caerulea*

# Chapter 8

# Tree Frogs

Tree frogs are some of the liveliest of all amphibians. They have sticky toe pads that allow them to climb just about any surface. This makes for a fascinating nighttime show when they are awake and active. There are dozens of different species of tree frogs available in the pet trade. In this chapter the care of four popular species is described.

## Natural History

The tree frog family Hylidae contains over 850 species of frogs, most of which are arboreal, spending their lives above ground in trees or other vegetation. To accommodate this lifestyle, tree frogs have sticky toe pads which allow them to climb. Most species are nocturnal and have enlarged eyes so they can see and hunt at night. They are agile predators, able to leap from a branch and catch insects in midflight.

During the day, tree frogs sleep and often conceal themselves in impressive ways. Some sleep stuck to the undersides of leaves, others live in water-filled tree holes. Most species can change color depending on the conditions in their environment. Light intensity, humidity levels, and temperature all contribute to the coloration a tree frog displays. Tree frogs are found worldwide, from temperate forests in North America to tropical jungles in Southeast Asia, and even in arid regions of South America.

Green tree frogs range from Delaware to eastern Texas and are common in North American pet stores.

White's tree frogs are often called dumpy tree frogs in the hobby. This is a species that is especially prone to becoming obese in captivity.

## Four Popular Tree Frogs

### Green Tree Frog

The green tree frog (*Hyla cinerea*) is native to the southeast United States, where it is common in swampy wetlands. Predominantly green in color, most also have a yellow or cream-colored lateral stripe running down their sides. Adults can grow to 2.0 inches (5.1 cm) in length. They are heavily collected for the pet trade and can be found for sale at just about any pet store in North

America that stocks herps. In captivity, green tree frogs are a pleasure keep, though their health must be carefully inspected upon acquisition to avoid purchasing weak or heavily stressed individuals.

## White's Tree Frog

One of the very best pet amphibians is White's tree frog (*Litoria caerulea*). These hefty Australian natives are both hardy and personable, seemingly posed with a constant smile. There are two "lines" of White's tree frogs available, one originating from Australia and the other from Indonesia. Australian White's tree frogs vary in color from turquoise to brown, while individuals from Indonesia are normally pear green to olive in color. Both are captive-bred in large numbers for the pet trade, though you'll also frequently find wild-caught adults from Indonesia for sale. Pass them up for captive-bred frogs when possible. Large White's tree frogs can reach 3.9 inches (10 cm) in length and need a bit more space than the other species discussed in this chapter.

## Cuban Tree Frog

A robust and lively species, the Cuban tree frog (*Osteopilus septentrionalis*) is an amusing frog to keep. Exceptionally large females have been known to reach more than 5.0 inches (12.7 cm) in length, while males may mature at only around 1.5 inches (3.8 cm). Cuban tree frogs are

White's tree frog is one the hardiest frogs. Additionally, it is not too difficult to breed, making it a great first species for aspiring frog breeders.

variable in coloration, capable of changing colors from tan to gray to white in a matter of minutes. A pattern of dark blotches often overlays this dorsal color. Native to various Caribbean islands, the species was unintentionally introduced into the United States. This has caused problems for many native amphibians because to the Cuban tree frog's appetite for other frogs as well as their mildly poisonous nature.

Cuban tree frogs are variable in color, ranging from yellowish to olive to brown. This one is greener in color than is typical.

### Red-Eyed Tree Frog

Familiar even to those who do not keep frogs, the red-eyed tree frog (*Agalychnis callidryas*) is regularly available from herp dealers and specialty pet stores. During the day these frogs conceal their colorful eyes, feet, and flanks to blend in with the underside of leaves under which they sleep. At night, blue and yellow striping is revealed on their body along with red eyes and orange feet. Male red-eyes grow to 2.0 inches (5.1 cm), while females are capable of reaching 3.0 inches (7.6 cm) in length. They are native to rainforests in Central America, with a large distribution that ranges from southern Mexico down to Colombia. In captivity, red-eyed tree frogs make sensitive but rewarding pets.

Selective captive breeding has produced a number of red-eyed tree frog color morphs. Xanthic individuals are yellow instead of green, with burgundy sides and white eyes. Albino red-eyes appear similar, but still retain crimson eyes. An unusual black form also exists, with not only black eyes but also charcoal dorsal coloration.

## Captive Care

### Acquisition

Tree frogs are widely available from pet stores, herp dealers, and breeders. White's tree frogs and red-eyed tree frogs are regularly bred in captivity. Opt for these captive-bred frogs over wild-caught frogs whenever possible. Green tree frogs and Cuban tree frogs are almost exclusively available in the form of wild-caught stock.

Examine the health of a tree frog before you purchase it. Rostral abrasions are not uncommon in these active amphibians. Also note the behavior. A healthy tree frog will normally be asleep above ground during the day, waking up only if food is available or if they are disturbed. To be safe, do not purchase a tree frog housed in an enclosure with others displaying symptoms of poor health, such as clouded eyes, skin sores, or unusual behavior.

## Housing

While tree frogs appear inactive during the day, they use all the room provided to them in captivity at night. A standard 15-gallon (56.8-l) aquarium is large enough for a trio of green tree frogs, red-eyed tree frogs, or other similarly-sized species. White's tree frogs and Cuban tree frogs need larger enclosures, with a 20-gallon

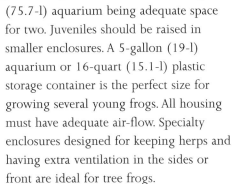

**A Background for Every Frog**

Consider attaching a background to the back and sides of glass enclosures. This prevents active or nervous tree frogs from trying to escape through the cage sides, reducing stress and preventing injury.

(75.7-l) aquarium being adequate space for two. Juveniles should be raised in smaller enclosures. A 5-gallon (19-l) aquarium or 16-quart (15.1-l) plastic storage container is the perfect size for growing several young frogs. All housing must have adequate air-flow. Specialty enclosures designed for keeping herps and having extra ventilation in the sides or front are ideal for tree frogs.

Within the enclosure, a substrate of moistened foam rubber, sphagnum moss, or coconut husk fiber works well. Use just enough to cover the bottom. Cage furnishings should include perches such as

Captive-bred red-eyed tree frogs are readily available and are much hardier than wild-caught ones.

driftwood, segments of PVC pipe, or plants (live or artificial). Pothos and Chinese evergreen are two good choices, though adult White's tree frogs may be a bit overpowering even for these sturdy species. Also include a shallow dish of amphibian-safe water. Some tree frogs are poor swimmers, so it's best if the water is no deeper than the frog itself is long.

Small tree frogs can also be housed in living terraria that incorporate numerous tropical plants and rely heavily on helpful microorganisms to control waste as it develops. Base your design around the species being kept. Red-eyed tree frogs appreciate large-leaved plants to sleep on during the day, while green tree frogs enjoy a pool of water with emergent vegetation, such as parrot's feather.

Tree frogs do well in tall enclosures with numerous perches and hiding places.

## Temperature and Humidity

Green tree frogs should be maintained between 72° and 80°F (22.2° and 26.7°C) during the day. The other three species covered in this chapter should be kept warmer, with one end of the enclosure approaching 85°F (29.4°C). This can be accomplished using a small infrared heat lamp. At night, allow the temperature to decrease by 5° to 10°F (3° to 6°C).

The humidity level in a tree frog enclosure is an important consideration. Generally it is better to have a slightly dry cage than an overly wet one. Tropical species like the red-eyed tree frog should have their cage misted with water daily to maintain an ambient humidity level of 60 to 100 percent. White's, Cuban, and green tree frogs are more tolerant of a variety of conditions, with average household humidity levels being adequate. For these species, mist the enclosure with water every other day to bring about temporary increases in humidity.

## Diet

The charisma with which tree frogs feed makes for an impressive show at night. Flying insects, such as house flies or moths, are particularly entertaining to feed to arboreal frogs. The staple diet for tree frogs, however, can be crickets. Two to six prey items per frog twice weekly is an adequate regimen for adults. Feed juvenile frogs nightly. Substitute other food items for crickets on a regular basis. Cockroaches and earthworms are good options. White's tree frogs and large Cuban tree frogs also accept pre-killed pinky mice from forceps. If used as food, mice should be fed only sparingly to avoid obesity. High-quality calcium and multivitamin supplements must be used on food items to prevent nutritional disorders from developing. Use supplements every other feeding for adults or on food each night for juveniles.

## Keeping It Clean

Tree frogs often rest on the side of the enclosure (as the red-eyed tree frog in the photo is doing) Shed skin and feces contribute to a film of bacteria that may cloud glass and give the tank a dirty look. Use a razor blade and distilled water to remove waste from the side of tree frog enclosures regularly.

# Breeding

## Sexing

In most species, male tree frogs are smaller than females and vocalize. Nuptial pads also develop on males, and if you see these you can be assured the frog is male. In White's tree frog, the size difference between sexes is not always obvious, so it's best to look at other features. Female White's tree frogs can also call, and often do so in response to a male, so watch their behavior at night to determine their sex.

Gray tree frogs (*Hyla chrysoscelis*) in amplexus. This species is slightly larger than the green tree frog, but its care is identical.

## Conditioning

To breed tree frogs in captivity, start by reducing the temperature to between 60° and 70°F (15.6° and 21.1°C). Lower humidity levels by cutting back on misting. The photoperiod can also be adjusted until there is light for only ten hours a day. Note that red-eyed tree frogs can be sensitive to cool temperatures and that instead of a reduction in temperature it is a decrease in humidity that is most important for conditioning this tropical species to breed.

After four to eight weeks of "winter," begin gradually warming the enclosure to the normal temperature range and start misting daily. Tree frogs become more active at this time and males begin to vocalize. It is crucial that tree frogs being conditioned be fed heavily; otherwise females will not have sufficient resources to develop eggs.

The red-eyed tree frogs is one of the species that lays its eggs on leaves overhanging water. When the tadpoles hatch, they fall into the water below.

## Rain Chamber and Egg Deposition

Once males are calling and females look fat, it is time to move tree frogs to a rain chamber. Heat the water to around 82°F (27.8°C). Outfit the rain chamber with a suitable area for egg deposition. Red-eyed tree frogs deposit eggs above water on smooth surfaces, so include broad-leafed plants for this purpose.

Anywhere from 11 to over 100 are laid. When you notice eggs, you can remove the leaf they are laid on and suspend it above water in an aquarium.

The other three species covered in this chapter scatter eggs about the surface of water, often draping them over emergent vegetation. Eggs can be left in the rain chamber to develop or removed to an aquarium once they hatch into tadpoles. Care for the tadpoles is as described in Chapter Four.

### More Males

**It is recommended to have extra males in a breeding group, as many as two to three times as many females. The competition between the males may help promote breeding success.**

*Rana pipiens*

# Chapter 9

# Bullfrogs, Leopard Frogs, and Other Frogs of the Genus *Rana*

**P**icture a stereotypical frog sitting on a lily pad. The image you have in your head probably resembles a member of the genus *Rana*. Commonly referred to as true frogs or pond frogs, *Rana* species have a familiar body structure with long legs, a streamlined body, and a pointed snout. Most are semi-aquatic and spend their time basking in sun near the water's edge. Water means security for these jumpy anurans, and they readily leap into it if startled or disturbed.

American bullfrogs are infamous for eating other frogs—just one reason introduced bullfrogs are serious threats to native frogs.

*Rana* species make nervous, jumpy captives, but with patience these long-legged semi-aquatic amphibians eventually tame down and adjust to life in captivity. Large enclosures are needed for most to fare well in the long term and must include a sizable filtered water area as well as access to land. Many keepers find enclosed greenhouses and ponds to work best. When provided with the right captive environment, *Rana* species will live many years and make enjoyable pets.

The genus *Rana* seems to constantly be under revision, with taxonomists splitting up and regrouping different species together into new genera as data on their evolutionary history becomes available. At the moment most would say there are around 90 *Rana* species, which range throughout the Americas, Europe, and Asia.

## Description of Commonly Available Species

### American Bullfrog

The American bullfrog (*Rana catesbeiana*) is a beastly amphibian. Large individuals have been known to grow to 8 inches (20.3 cm) in length, though even at a more common adult size of around 6 inches (15.2 cm) bullfrogs appear supersized. They have strong hind limbs, for which they are farmed in huge numbers, appearing on restaurant menus around the world. Coloration varies from olive to grass green, sometimes with erratic spotting. An albino form is also available, being golden yellow with red eyes. Because of their size and powerful jumping ability, bullfrogs require especially large enclosures.

The native distribution of the bullfrog spans eastern North America, as far north as southern Quebec and southwards into Veracruz, Mexico. Due to both intentional and unintentional releases, populations of American bullfrogs can now be found just about everywhere, from California to the Amazon, in Italy, and even parts of Asia. In many places bullfrogs have had a devastating effect on native amphibians because of their predatory nature and the foreign pathogens they introduce to local frog populations.

## Bronze Frog

Resembling a small American bullfrog, the bronze frog (*Rana clamitans*) grows to between 2.5 and 4 inches (6.4 and 10.2 cm). Juveniles are often spotted in black dots, which may or may not fade as the frog matures. These dots are patterned over a background color that usually falls somewhere between muddy brown and asparagus green. There are two subspecies. *R. c. clamitans* is commonly called the bronze frog and ranges throughout the southeast United States. *R. c. melanota* is found farther north and is usually called the green frog. Care for both is similar, though it is helpful to know the origin of individuals so that appropriate seasonal variations in temperature can be provided.

## Leopard Frogs

There are a handful of different leopard frog species in North America. All share a sharp pattern of dark spots on their dorsum, which stand out between two prominent dorsolateral ridges. The northern leopard frog (*R. pipiens*) and southern leopard frog (*R. sphenocephala*) are occasionally available through pet dealers, though they are more commonly encountered in a classroom when ordered from biological supply companies. Both species grow to between 2 and 5 inches (5.1 and 12.7 cm), and are typically quite high-strung captives, bounding into the water when startled by movement outside the enclosure.

## Chytrid Carrier

Some American bullfrogs are able to live with the deadly chytrid fungus that is causing catastrophic amphibian population declines and extinctions. Because they are farmed in great numbers for their legs and shipped worldwide, it is thought they may be one of the ways the amphibian chytrid fungus is spreading.

## European Common Frog

Familiar to those who live in Europe, R. *temporaria* is often kept by children or used for educational purposes. Its coloration is a variable shade of brown, sometimes with yellowish tones, especially in females. Adults grow to 3 inches (7.6 cm) in length. Their range extends up to the Arctic Circle, and depending on the population, the European common frog can be quite tolerant of the cold. It is best kept in outdoor enclosures. If it is kept indoors, use a semi-aquatic setup that incorporates a larger land area than that designed for the North American species described above.

The green frog, a subspecies of the bronze frog, is abundant throughout most of its range. It is somewhat adaptable to disturbed habitat as long as there is water present.

## Asian Ranids

Various ranids from Asia are sporadically imported, and although recently removed from the genus *Rana*, most sport a body structure and semi-aquatic life history similar to the familiar true frogs of North America and Europe.

The green-backed frog (*Hylarana erythraea*) is occasionally available. Most grow to between 1.6 and 3 inches (4.0 and 7.5 cm) and are patterned much like a green-colored leopard frog without spots. They inhabit ponds and rice paddies throughout Southeast Asia.

The Malaysian fire frog (*Hylarana signata*) is an infrequently imported but beautiful ranid from Thailand, Malaysia, and Indonesia. On top of the black body are two orange dorsolateral stripes, around which are yellow-orange spots and blotches. This species is slightly smaller than the green-backed frog. As a tropical streamside species, the Malaysian fire frog should be offered moving water in captivity along with a sizable land area that includes plenty of cover.

## Captive Care

*Rana* species can be difficult to maintain. While tadpoles are easy to grow and small juvenile frogs can be kept simply, adults are powerful jumpers and require plenty of space. If a keeper can create and maintain a suitably large enclosure, the rest of their care is rather simple.

## Acquisition

Unlike most other pet frogs, *Rana* species are more often encountered in their larval stage than as adults. Pet stores in North America regularly stock American bullfrog, bronze frog, and leopard frog tadpoles—often with no identification. Biological supply companies that supply schools are also a common source for tadpoles and frogs. Collecting individuals from the wild is another way to acquire *Rana* species, though wild-caught frogs make particularly nervous captives. First make sure this is legal to do in your area (a permit may be required), and remember to never release a wild frog once it has been kept in captivity.

*Rana* tadpoles are not especially active, so don't worry if those at a store simply rest on the bottom of the aquarium. They should swim frantically, however, if disturbed, so pass up lethargic individuals that do not move away from an approaching net. Examine adult frogs for rostral abrasions, which commonly occur in small, overstocked enclosures at pet stores, and avoid purchasing any frog that looks thin or is in an enclosure with others that show signs of poor health.

## Housing

The best way to house a group of *Rana* is in a greenhouse with a pond. This must be completely enclosed so that frogs cannot escape and planted with emergent vegetation to provide cover at the water's edge. Natural seasonal variation in temperature and photoperiod may promote breeding in the spring, which is enjoyable to observe.

Not everyone has access to a yard or enough space to provide secure outdoor housing, so aquariums can be used instead. A standard 30-gallon (113.6-l) aquarium is enough room for a pair of leopard frogs or a similarly sized species. Use only the largest of aquariums to house big *Rana* species such as bullfrogs. Tape an aquarium background or dark-colored paper to three of the glass sides. Better housing options—especially for large individuals—are stock tanks, cattle troughs,

Southern leopard frogs usually have a white spot on the tympanum, which distinguishes them from northern leopards.

The green-backed frog (left) and the Malaysian fire frog (right) are two Southeast Asian ranids that show up in the pet trade on occasion. Keep them slightly warmer than the other frogs discussed in this chapter.

and large plastic storage containers. These enclosures offer more room than many aquariums, especially in width, and the opaque sides help prevent nervous frogs from getting spooked and harming themselves in an attempt to escape. Modify plastic containers with a homemade cover that offers plenty of ventilation.

As evident from the webbing on their feet, *Rana* species are excellent swimmers. One way to create an appropriate semi-aquatic setup is to fill an aquarium two-thirds full with water and then position driftwood and large rocks so that they break the water's surface, providing access to land. Towards one end of the tank aim a small heat lamp at an island of rocks or driftwood pile to provide a basking spot that is slightly warmer than the rest of the cage. A bare-bottom underwater stratum makes cleanup quick and simple. If gravel is used instead, make sure to siphon out waste regularly with an aquarium vacuum. Good filtration is a must, with an appropriately sized power filter doing the job; a canister filter can be especially effective.

When housing juvenile frogs, *Rana* species that are more terrestrial than aquatic (such as the European common frog [R. temporaria] or wood frog [R. sylvatica]), or when temporary housing is needed, a simple setup consisting of a layer of sphagnum moss, a large water dish, and several pieces of driftwood may work better than the aquatic setup described above.

## Temperature and Humidity

Able to hibernate under frigid water during winter but also bask in the summer sun, *Rana* from temperate regions are quite tolerant in regard to temperature. Other than a spot lamp positioned over a section of land, heating is rarely needed. Maintain the enclosure between 65° and 77°F (18.3° and 25°C) for American bullfrogs, bronze frogs, and leopard frogs, and several degrees cooler for European common frogs. At night, the temperature should decrease by 10°F (6°C). In addition to these moderate temperatures, *Rana* species live well within average household humidity levels. Tropical Asian species should be kept warmer, above 70°F (21°C), and with less fluctuation in temperature.

## Diet

*Rana* are voracious predators. American bullfrogs have been known to eat rodents, birds, and snakes. Captive frogs accept a variety of foods, and some can be weaned onto pellet diets if the pellets are first offered in a dish mixed with live prey. Movement generally triggers a feeding response, with live crickets, earthworms, and night crawlers forming a good staple diet. Feeder fish or pre-killed rodents offered with forceps can also be fed occasionally.

Juveniles should be fed daily, while adult *Rana* can be fed twice a week, with two to six food items per frog being adequate. If frogs are kept at cooler temperatures during winter months, feeding frequency must be reduced. Use high-quality multivitamin and calcium supplements to help prevent nutritional deficiencies from developing.

## Breeding

Outside of commercial frog farms and conservation projects, *Rana* species are rarely bred in captivity. This is understandable, because it takes quite a bit of work to raise tadpoles, and the demand for captive-bred *Rana* is small except for food markets. Before starting a breeding project, first carefully consider what you will do with the resulting offspring. To avoid introducing harmful pathogens to local amphibian populations, never release captive frogs into the wild.

## Timid Eaters

If there is movement outside the cage or if people are watching, newly acquired *Rana* may refuse to eat. Be patient. After several months in captivity most adjust and may even begin to associate the opening of their cage with food.

## Sexing

*Rana* can be sexed in the spring breeding season by listening for calling males. In certain species, males have a yellow throat. Additionally, examine the front digits for nuptial pads. If these darkened rough surfaces are present, the frog is male. Size can also be helpful in determining sex. Females may be larger or more heavyset than males. The tympanum of a female may also be smaller than that of a male. A good breeding group consists of at least three males for every female.

## Captive Breeding

*Rana* breed most often in captivity when kept in an enclosed outdoor pond. The natural variation in temperature and photoperiod outside help promote breeding behavior. When males start calling in the spring and early summer months, feed heavily so that females produce eggs. If breeding is successful, tadpoles can be removed and kept in small groups within aquaria so that they do not overpopulate the pond.

European common frog with her clutch of eggs. Most ranid species lay hundereds or thousands of eggs at a time.

If attempting to breed *Rana* species indoors, you will need a large enclosure that can house a group of frogs, such as a cattle trough. Re-create seasonal variation in temperature by keeping the enclosure in a cool location and then heating it during spring and summer. Frogs that come from cooler locations may need a stronger contrast in temperature between winter and summer, possibly even a period of hibernation. In addition to temperature, manipulate the photoperiod by placing lights on an electrical timer so that during winter the frogs receive only eight to ten hours of daylight.

Females deposit eggs around aquatic vegetation in large jellylike masses. A clutch of leopard frog or bronze frog eggs may number more than 3,000, while

## Long Larval Stage

Bullfrog tadpoles may take up to three years to complete metamorphosis in the wild, overwintering through two winters. In a heated aquarium their metabolism speeds up and front legs normally emerge before they are six months old.

American bullfrogs have been known to produce as many as 20,000 eggs. These hatch into tadpoles in under a week at warmer temperatures or may take several weeks to develop when kept cool.

## Tadpole Care

A standard 10-gallon aquarium (38-l) is large enough for four or five tadpoles. Heavily filtered stock tanks are needed to raise the hundreds that result from a successful captive breeding. See Chapter 4 for more housing ideas. Wild *Rana* tadpoles often seek shallow water in the sun where it is warm, swimming away to cold deeper depths only when disturbed. Use a submersible aquarium heater to maintain a water temperature between 72° and 80°F (22.2° and 26.7°C). At this warm temperature range, tadpoles typically complete metamorphosis in three to six months.

Tadpoles of *Rana* species are largely herbivores, so feed a diet of commercially available tadpole food, boiled greens, and algae-based fish foods. Once front arms develop and the tail begins to be absorbed, provide access to land by floating a piece of cork bark or Styrofoam in the water. This prevents drowning. Offer crickets or other live invertebrate prey to the young frogs several days after the tail is completely absorbed.

Male ranids typically have much larger tympanums than the females, as seen on this male bullfrog.

*Bufo cognatus*

# Chapter 10

# True Toads:
# The Family Bufonidae

There are more than 500 species in the family Bufonidae, members of which are commonly called true toads. They make some of the most personable of all captive anurans, posed with a timeless expression on their face and wise eyes. Contrary to popular belief, toads won't give you warts. Instead, their bumpy or warty look results from numerous skin glands. Toads adjust well to life in captivity but can be secretive during the day because they are nocturnal.

## Description of Commonly Available Species

### Southern Toad and Related Species

Native to the southeastern United States, the southern toad (*Bufo terrestris*) lives in a variety of habitats and may even be found in residential areas hunting insects that gather near light sources at night. Adults range in size from 1.6 to 4.5 inches (4.1 to 11.4 cm). They have a typical toad look, with brown bumpy skin, noticeable parotid glands at the base of the head, and a lightly colored dorsal stripe that extends down the back. Some individuals tend towards red or black in coloration. Southern toads are available sporadically from pet stores and dealers, along with a few other North American species like the American toad (*Bufo americanus*) and the tiny diurnal oak toad (*B. quercicus*). A particularly notable and often available North American toad is the colorful western green toad (*B. debilis*), which is clad in yellow-green with black reticulations. All make hardy captives when acquired in good condition.

The southern toad ranges across the southeastern United States and is most abundant in areas with sandy soil.

### European Green Toad

The green toad (*Bufo viridis*) has a striking pattern of green on tan, the hue of which varies between individuals. It matures at between 2.5 and 4.0 inches (6.4 and 10.2 cm). Green toads have a wide range throughout Europe and northern Africa, so wide in fact that upon recent analysis of distant populations many taxonomists now consider the green toad to be composed of several different species. In the North American pet trade, most individuals come from Egypt. Here they occupy a variety of habitats, from scrubland and forested areas to desert oases.

### Smooth-Sided Toad

Of the tropical *Bufo* species, the smooth-sided toad (*Bufo guttatus*) is one of the most elegantly patterned. The dorsum is tan or cream, usually with clusters of dark raised bumps. This dorsal coloration contrasts sharply with the brick-red flanks. Smooth-sided toads are large, with big females approaching 10 inches (25.4 cm). Males are smaller, but still hefty at 6 inches (15.2 cm). They range throughout the Amazon, where they spend their time in leaf litter on the forest floor, often near streams or rivers.

## Marine Toad

Marine toads (*Bufo marinus*) are massive, growing to over 10 inches (25.4 cm) in length. They are native to Central and South America, though they are now known as an invasive species around the world due to the experimental release of marine toads as a pest control measure in the first half of the last century (it did not work). In captivity, marine toads make impressive captives, with huge parotoid glands and a beastly appetite to match their large size. Individuals in the pet trade often come from the invasive Florida population, but big adults are also imported from Central America with some frequency.

## Asian Black-Spined Toad

The Asian black-spined or spiny toad (*Duttaphrynus melanostictus*) is periodically imported and makes a hardy captive. It is attractively

European green toads can be found in many different habitats from forests to deserts.

# Tree Toads

Not all toads are terrestrial. *Pedostibes hosii*, the yellow-spotted climbing toad, has enlarged toe pads and spends its time above ground near tropical forest streams in Borneo, Sumatra, Malaysia, and Thailand. These tree toads are sexually dimorphic. Beautiful yellow-spotted green females measure 4 inches (10.2 cm) and are nearly twice the size of the reddish brown males. Occasionally imported, yellow-spotted climbing toads can be maintained in large arboreal enclosures with high levels of humidity and plenty of vegetation for cover. They are notoriously difficult to acclimate to captivity, so upon acquisition it's best to quarantine them individually while consulting a veterinarian about appropriate treatment for likely parasite infections.

patterned, with a series of black speckling and dots covering the body, which itself varies from golden tan to deep brown with hints of red or burgundy. Their exotic appearance is paired with a moderate size. Most individuals grow to around 3.5 inches (8.9 cm). This toad has a large distribution throughout Southeast Asia, where it occupies many different environments, from the edges of rainforest to fields in small towns.

## Bumblebee Walking Toads

Toads of the genus *Melanophryniscus* are sporadically imported from South America. They are attractively patterned in contrasting yellow and black dorsally, complemented with bright crimson underneath, especially on their feet and near the vent. With males maturing at around 1.0 inch (2.5 cm) and females growing only slightly larger, bumblebee walking toads make fine captives for a small terrarium.

Do not keep these toads overly wet. Although their exotic coloration may evoke images of lush tropical rainforests, bumblebee walking toads are native to dry grasslands in Argentina, Paraguay, and extreme southern Brazil, and only experience wet and humid conditions for a small part of each year. Species imported in the recent past appear to include *M. fulvoguttatus*,

M. *klappenbachi*, and M. *stelzneri*, but there is some confusion regarding the variation between different imports.

# Captive Care

## Acquisition

True toads can be acquired through pet stores, but most species are available only periodically. At certain times of the year it may be difficult to locate particular species. Check with dealers if looking for a group of toads that can't be found locally. Collection is also a popular way to acquire true toads. Most every part of the world has a local *Bufo* species or two. (Only the introduced marine toad is found in Australia and New Guinea.) They are regularly encountered at night, sometimes in urban areas. If collecting a toad, be careful to first make sure it is legal to do so. Permits may be required. Also, never release a collected toad back into the wild.

## Housing

Toads do not require complex housing and can be maintained in simple setups. An aquarium lined with moist paper towels, a piece or two of cork bark, and a water dish can be used to permanently keep many bufonids. Burrowing comes naturally to toads, so alternatively a mixture of coconut husk fiber and sand can be used as the substrate. Offer food in a shallow dish to prevent toads from ingesting substrate mixtures. Many toads learn to wait near this dish at night for food. In

The smooth-sided toad is a large and impressive amphibian. The individuals in the pet trade are usually wild-caught and imported from Suriname, although Colombia exported them in the past.

Marine toads often have enormous parotoid glands full of toxins to ward off predators. Handled gently, they will not secrete these chemicals.

enclosures housing smaller species, you can grow hardy live plants like pothos.

Cage size depends on the species being kept. A standard 15-gallon (56.8-l) aquarium is enough space for two southern toads, European green toads, or similar-sized species. Jumbo marine toads and smooth-sided toads require substantially more room to live, with large plastic storage containers forming perfect housing. Aquariums can also be used to house large toads. A 40-gallon (151.4-l) "breeder" aquarium provides room for a pair. Use a screen cover rather than a glass lid to offer adequate ventilation.

## Deep Dishes

Pay special attention to the depth of the water dish. Deep water dishes or those that are difficult for toads to access may pose a drowning risk. Place several rocks in a water dish to make it easy for the toad to move in and out.

The water source and moisture in the enclosure is an important consideration. All toads enjoy soaking in water at night, and water used this way must be changed each morning so that it stays fresh. Also important is the moisture content of the substrate. Toads from arid or temperate regions do not tolerate soggy conditions. Consider providing a moisture gradient throughout the cage, with an area of slightly moist soil or moss on one side, and another end where the substrate is dry.

## Temperature and Humidity

True toads are hardy creatures that tolerate a wide range of temperatures. North American species from temperate regions, such as the southern toad or American toad, are best kept cool, with a daytime temperature that only approaches 75°F (24°C). This should drop at night by 10° to 15°F (6° to 9°C). Green toads thrive within a similar temperature range, although they need it a bit warmer at night. Toads from tropical and subtropical climates, like the smooth-sided, marine, and black-spined toads, should be kept warm. Provide a temperature range between 70° and 82°F (21.1° and 27.8°C) for these species. A low-power infrared heat lamp can be used to heat the cage and also allows you to view the toads at night when they are active.

Bumblebee walking toads should not be kept in overly high humidity. They are from dry grasslands and only experience humid conditions during the rainy season.

Average household humidity levels between 35 and 60 percent are appropriate for keeping most toads. If keeping tropical species, mist the enclosure with water each day to bring about temporary increases in humidity.

## Diet

Although toads can be shy, all readily emerge from hiding to hunt prey at night. Crickets and earthworms can form the bulk of the diet. Offer two to six per toad twice a week. Night crawlers are especially useful for feeding large individuals. Other foods such as mealworms, superworms, wax worms, and cockroaches can be substituted for crickets and earthworms every couple of weeks. Marine and smooth-sided toads also eat rodents, but rodents should be fed sparingly, if at all. Coat food lightly in a nutritional supplement every other feeding or at each feeding for juvenile toads.

## Hand Feeding

Once adjusted to their enclosure, many toads accept food from the hand. Feeding by hand is fun and also helps monitor exactly how much each toad is eating and prevents them from accidentally ingesting substrate.

# Breeding

Toads are rarely the focus of captive breeding projects outside of conservation initiatives. This is unfortunate, especially for some of the oddball tropical species that are infrequently imported.

Male toads can be told apart from females by their smaller size and ability to call. The throats of males that have been calling darken in color. Additionally, nuptial pads develop on males when in breeding condition.

Seasonal cycles are most important for conditioning toads to breed, but the severity of the seasons depends on the species of toad and its natural habitat. Toads from less severe climates may only need a month or two of cool temperatures (about 50°F [10°C]), as would be experienced if the cage is placed in a basement for a few weeks of the year. If attempting to breed tropical species, try cutting back on misting for several months and letting the substrate of the cage dry while maintaining normal temperatures.

Pair of Asian black-spined toads in amplexus. This species is not often captive-bred.

Some species require a period of hibernation during which they are cooled to 40°F (4.4°C) for one month. Toads can be placed in ventilated plastic storage containers lined with damp sandy soil and moss and placed in the refrigerator. During this time they do not require food, but it's important they are monitored frequently and that the substrate does not completely dry. Hibernation is stressful and there is often mortality in a breeding group. Feed toads heavily prior to reducing temperatures this low, but do not feed the week prior to hibernation so that they empty their gut.

Following a simulated winter or dry period, toads should be returned to normal conditions for a week or two and fed nightly. Mist each day, and when males begin to call at night move them to a rain chamber, followed by females a day or two later. Most species lay eggs in long strings, often around aquatic vegetation. Females often produce many thousands of eggs, with a single female marine toad able to deposit 30,000 eggs. The small black tadpoles that result are hardy, feeding well on fish flakes, boiled greens, and algae. Some toads may complete metamorphosis quickly—under a month when kept in warm water. Others may take several months, especially if they are raised in unheated aquariums

Underside of a bumblebee walking toad, showing the dramatic red colors. When threatened, the toad will arch its back to reveal the red warning colors.

New metamorphs are tiny, often 0.5 inches (1.3 cm) or less. Feed hatchling crickets and flightless fruit flies to them daily, coated in appropriate nutritional supplements at each feeding. At this small size, toads are prone to desiccation, so ensure that the substrate does not completely dry and that there is always a source of shallow water available.

Pipa pipa

# Chapter 11

# Aquatic Frogs: The Family Pipidae

B oth the African clawed frog and African dwarf frog are popular aquarium pets. These fully aquatic amphibians are commonly available from the fish department of pet stores and are easily cared for. A third aquatic species, the Suriname toad, is sporadically available in the form of wild-caught imports from South America. All of these aquatic species are somewhat unconventional pet frogs and make fine captives when set up in the correct environment.

African clawed frogs are extremely hardy, so hardy that they have become invasive in numerous areas far outside their natural range.

## Description of Species

### African Clawed Frog

A native of southern Africa, the African clawed frog (*Xenopus laevis*) is large and unusual. African clawed frogs have a roughly triangular body, with powerful hind limbs for swimming as well as claws on their toes. Large individuals can grow to 5 inches (12.7 cm) in length. Their natural dorsal coloration is mottled brown and gray, but more often albino individuals are available that are colored off-white. In my mind, the smooth skin, body shape, and color of albino clawed frogs are a bit evocative of a raw chicken breast. These are strange animals that make hardy pets. In addition to being popular in the pet trade, they have also been used heavily for research.

### African Dwarf Frogs

As their name implies, African dwarf frogs (*Hymenochirus boettgeri* and *H. curtipes*) are small amphibians. The biggest individuals grow to just 1.4 inches (3.5 cm). They are predominantly gray or brown in color, with small granulated dots covering the body. African dwarf frogs are native to central Africa, where they inhabit shaded rainforest pools. Other popular trade names include dwarf water frog, underwater frog, and dwarf African clawed frog. Two dwarf frog species are available but are difficult to tell apart. Most often H. *boettgeri* is found for sale, though H. *curtipes* may also be available and is said to have "more granulated skin" as well as hind limbs that are shorter than those of H. *boettgeri*. Care for both is identical.

## Suriname Toad

There are few frogs more bizarre in appearance than the Suriname toad (*Pipa pipa*). It is dorsoventrally flattened, with an angled head, gigantic mouth, and two minute pinhole eyes. Though they often use fleshy points on their face and fingers to feel their way around, Suriname toads also have fairly good eyesight. Adults range from 4 inches (10.2 cm) to 8 inches (20.3 cm), and at this size require large aquaria. They are native to murky waters of northern South America, where they spend much of their time sifting through debris on the bottom of rivers for small fish and crustaceans.

# Captive Care

African clawed frogs and African dwarf frogs are easy to maintain in captivity. The Suriname toad can be a bit more challenging because of its size and the lack of captive-bred stock. All of these aquatic frogs become quite personable with time, learning to beg for food and to be hand-fed at the water's surface.

## Acquisition

African clawed and dwarf frogs are regularly available in the fish department of pet stores. Clawed frogs can also be obtained through biological supply companies or classroom settings, where their tadpoles are grown to study the amphibian life cycle. Both species are generally found for sale in good health, but they should be examined carefully for signs of disease, such as red spotting, lesions, or lethargic behavior. Suriname toads are less commonly encountered at pet stores than the African species because they are rarely bred in captivity. Instead, P. *pipa* individuals are more often available from dealers at reptile shows.

## An Unusual Pregnancy Test

When female African clawed frogs are injected with the urine of a pregnant woman they develop eggs in response to her hormones. These frogs were among the first pregnancy tests, gaining popularity during the 1940's.

Suriname toads require large aquariums and prefer subdued lighting. In nature, they live at the bottom of sluggish, murky waters.

There is increased concern about aquatic frogs being carriers of the amphibian chytrid fungus, which seems a likely cause of mortality at pet stores and dealers. If any individuals in a tank appear lethargic, are spending time out of water, or seem to be shedding their skin excessively, find another source for your frogs.

## Housing

Pipids are aquatic amphibians and rarely leave the water, so use an aquarium for housing. Frogs will escape through gaps in the lid, so take care that the top is secure. A standard 10-gallon (38-l) aquarium offers enough room for four African dwarf frogs or a pair of African clawed frogs. Suriname toads are larger amphibians and should be offered as much space as possible. Two can be kept successfully in a 30-gallon (113.6-l) aquarium, but a standard 55-gallon (208.2-l) tank that offers 4 feet (1.2 m) of swimming room is a better option.

An aquarium setup for aquatic frogs is similar to that of one for tropical fish. Gravel provides surface area for beneficial bacteria to colonize as well as footing for frogs. The gravel should be too large for frogs to swallow. In temporary setups or quarantine situations a bare bottom can be used instead. Offer a water depth between 10 inches (25.4 cm) and 20 inches (50.8 cm). Within the aquarium there should be hiding spots and visual barriers, such as driftwood or rock structures.

Live plants are a great way to provide cover. African clawed frogs and Suriname toads tend to uproot and disturb all but the hardiest of species, so try using clumps of java moss for these robust amphibians. Floating vegetation like giant salvinia and Amazon frogbit are particularly useful in aquariums housing aquatic frogs. They diffuse light, which reduces algal growth and helps aquatic frogs feel secure. Housing for African dwarf frogs can be made more attractive by use of a variety of low-light-tolerant aquatic plants. Tropical fish stores should have a selection of suitable plants.

Proper filtration is crucial to maintaining water quality. Power filters that hang over the back are ideal for small tanks, while canister filters are the best option for larger aquariums. Regular partial water changes must be performed to keep the frogs in good health. At a minimum, replace 30 percent of the water every other week. Avoid complete water changes because replacing all of the water can shock frogs and harm beneficial microorganisms that control their waste.

# Frogs and Fish

It's best to keep aquatic frogs separate from fish. African clawed frogs and Suriname toads will eat other aquarium inhabitants, while dwarf frogs are often outcompeted for food when part of a community aquarium. There is also the possibility that the amphibians' skin toxins are detrimental to fish.

African clawed frogs and other pipids eat many of the same foods that tropical fish do, such as bloodworms.

## Temperature

African clawed frogs fare best when kept between 68° and 76°F (20° and 24.4°C). African dwarf frogs and Suriname toads are sensitive to low temperatures, so maintain these species closer to 80°F (26.7°C). A fully submersible thermostatically equipped aquarium heater can be used to heat the water. Glass heaters are fragile and easily crack. Plastic or metal heaters are better options. To avoid burning frogs, use a heater designed for use with aquatic turtles that comes with a plastic guard. Frogs may find the gap between standard heaters and side of the aquarium to be the perfect resting spot, but when the temperature of the water cools and the heater turns on it can cause severe burns.

## Diet

Aquatic frogs are easy to feed. They eat live foods with enthusiasm, while they also accept prepared frog diets. This makes feeding a cinch for keepers who remain uneasy about feeding live prey. Offer food to juvenile frogs daily and to adults twice a week.

African dwarf frogs are small amphibians and require similarly small food. Blackworms, chopped earthworms, and daphnia are relished. These live foods are perfect for getting picky eaters started. Mix in frozen bloodworms, *Tubifex* worms, and small sinking fish foods for variety. If you are keeping dwarf frogs with fish, their food may be eaten by the fish before they notice it. To help counter this problem, feed fish first in one half of the aquarium, and while they are distracted offer food to the frogs on the other side of the tank.

African clawed frogs and Suriname toads feed on larger foods than dwarf frogs. Live night crawlers, feeder fish, freshwater shrimp, and small crayfish all work well. If using feeder fish, do not rely solely on goldfish and instead mix minnows and guppies into the diet to avoid nutritional disorders. Small strips of beef heart and liver are also accepted when offered with forceps, but should be fed rarely, if at all. Commercially available pellet foods designed for amphibians are also regularly accepted by African clawed frogs.

## Breeding

The abundance of captive-bred African clawed frogs in the pet trade is a result of hormone-induced breeding at commercial facilities. It is not difficult, however, to breed these frogs naturally by manipulating water depth and temperature. Sometimes breeding even occurs accidentally following a water change. African dwarf frogs are less often bred by hobbyists, but by adjusting water temperature and other aspects of their environment, *Hymenochirus* can also be bred without much difficulty. Suriname toads have a unique breeding strategy that is detailed separately.

## Sexing

African clawed frogs are easily sexed by examining two features. First look at size. Females are usually larger than males. Next, look between their legs. Mature males have small fleshy protuberances called papillae around the cloaca (vent).

African dwarf frogs can be a bit more difficult to sex. Body structure differs between males and females, and in mature, well-fed frogs, females appear more heavyset than the smaller and more streamlined males. It is also reported that males have a larger tympanum (ear) than females, though this can be difficult to see.

African clawed frogs generally scatter their eggs around the aquarium; sometimes the eggs will adhere to plants, as seen here.

In Suriname toads, it is also thought that males are smaller than females. A better way to determine the sex of *Pipa pipa* is to examine the cloaca. In males it is "pointed" and "downturned," while in females the cloaca is "thicker" and "upturned."

Perhaps the best way to sex all of these aquatic frogs is to listen. Males produce sharp clicking calls year-round, usually at night. If a frog calls, it is unquestionably male.

## Breeding African Clawed Frogs and African Dwarf Frogs

African dwarf frogs require higher temperatures than their larger relatives.

The African pipids regularly breed in captivity when water depth, temperature, and light intensity are manipulated. Start by reducing the water level, through both evaporation and manual water removal. At the same time, turn the thermostat up on the aquarium heater to raise the temperature until it approaches 85°F (29.4°C). Light intensity can also be increased by adding additional fluorescent lighting over the tank.

African clawed frog tadpoles have sensory tentacles at the front of the head, presumably to help them find food.

By changing their environment in this way you are replicating the dry season in Africa, during which time rains cease, water bodies dry up, and the water temperature increases. It may be beneficial to keep males separate from females during this simulated dry season.

After several weeks, perform a partial water change and return frogs to normal conditions. Some hobbyists recommend using cool water when increasing the water depth to replicate the conditions frogs experience as their drying pools are flooded with rainwater. Maintain a constant water temperature near 80°F (26.7°C) for dwarf frogs, and closer to 75°F (24°C) for clawed frogs. If well fed, females swell with eggs and males will soon amplex them.

African dwarf frogs deposit eggs near the surface of the water, with pairs floating upside down together at the top of the aquarium. They lay as many as 1,000 pinhead-sized eggs. African clawed frogs produce greater numbers of eggs, which they scatter about the aquarium floor. Infertile eggs usually develop fungus and appear blurry within the first day. Separate these from fertile eggs as soon as you notice them.

Tadpoles are largely filter feeders, and when they first hatch from the egg they require tiny suspended food particles in the water to survive. Liquid foods designed for raising fish fry can be used at this early stage. You may also try inoculating water with infusorians (microscopic planktonic organisms) that are either from a local pond or have been cultured in a clear water-filled container sitting outside in sun. Once tadpoles put on size they readily eat fish flake foods that have been ground into a powder. Live baby brine shrimp and daphnia are also accepted. Tadpoles complete metamorphosis between four and six weeks, and once the tail is absorbed they can be fed the same food that is fed to adults, only smaller.

## Breeding Suriname Toads

Suriname toads employ a fascinating reproductive strategy. The eggs brood in a spongy tissue on the female's back and hatch directly into miniature adults. Males may engage females in amplexus for several days before breeding occurs. As eggs are expelled and fertilized, the pair does a series of turns and flips in the water until eggs adhere to the back of the female. From here, tissue swells around each egg. Sixty to 200 eggs are deposited on her back; they take between 11 and 20 weeks to develop into fully formed but tiny Suriname toads.

While fresh imports frequently engage in amplexus, it is rare for egg deposition to take place in captivity, let alone for eggs to develop into young that survive. Similar temperature, photoperiod, and water level manipulation as described for the African pipids above may help coax pairs of Suriname toads to breed. If breeding is successful, the female and her developing young must be monitored carefully. Dead froglets should be manually removed from the female's back to prevent infection. Young Suriname toads still on the back of the female move around and can even feed on small prey during the last stages of development. Once they are free swimming, remove froglets to a separate aquarium and offer a diet of blackworms, *Tubifex* worms, brine shrimp, small guppies, and other suitably sized live aquatic prey.

## Invasive Frogs

Released African clawed frogs have established populations in the Americas and Europe, disturbing aquatic ecosystems and causing problems for native amphibians. Never let clawed frogs go into the wild. Instead, return them to the place they were purchased if you can no longer keep them.

African clawed frog tadpoles take four to six weeks to metamorphose into froglets.

Mantella viridis

# Chapter 12

# Other Frogs and Toads

A book of this size cannot cover all frogs and toads, but included here are guidelines for keeping some of the more commonly encountered oddball species not discussed in previous chapters. Many of these frogs are available only as wild-caught imports. This is in part caused by the lack of attention given to them by institutions and experienced private breeders, but can also be attributed to the unique breeding behaviors of some of these anurans that make them tricky to breed in captivity.

## Tomato Frog

The Madagascar-endemic genus *Dyscophus* contains three species commonly called tomato frogs. *D. guineti* is the only one regularly available, and it inhabits tropical forests and swampy areas in the eastern half of the island. These frogs are well deserving of their common name, with a round body and coloration that varies between orange-red and beautiful crimson. Sometimes a weak reticulated pattern is apparent over this background color. Male *D. guineti* grow to 2.5 inches (6.4 cm) and tend more towards yellow, while the redder females are capable of reaching 3.7 inches (9.4 cm). During the day tomato frogs are quite secretive and burrow to avoid detection. They are great fun to watch at night, however, as they slowly creep around their tank to hunt prey. A 10-gallon (38-l) aquarium is enough room for a pair. This should be lined with a layer of moist sphagnum moss, coconut husk fiber, or a mixture of the two. Provide cover with artificial plants or pieces of cork bark, as well as a small water dish. Tomato frogs are tropical amphibians and should be kept warm, between 75°and 82°F (24° and 27.8°C) during the day, dropping by 5°F (3°C) at night. Mist the enclosure daily to maintain humidity levels between 70 and 90 percent.

Tomato frogs are hardy, colorful frogs. Captive-bred froglets are sometimes available at reptile shows and through online vendors.

## A Sticky Defense

When tomato frogs are threatened they puff up with air. If continually harassed, they release from skin glands a sticky white substance that deters predators from eating them.

Feeding is rarely a problem for tomato frogs, though recently imported individuals may refuse to eat in the open while acclimating to captivity. Crickets can form the staple diet. Offer two to five per frog twice a week. Small earthworms, wax worms, silkworms, and other invertebrate prey are also greedily eaten from a feeding dish at night. Juvenile tomato frogs must be fed smaller food, like flightless fruit flies and small crickets. Coat food in appropriate nutritional supplements every other feeding for adults and at nearly every meal for growing juveniles.

Breeding occurs in captivity, but it is often induced through the use of hormones. The persistent hobbyist can also breed tomato frogs with a more natural method of replicating seasonal cycles. To replicate a dry season, lower the humidity by increasing ventilation and reducing mistings. Allow the substrate to dry some, but ensure that there is always a source of water available. Following several months of this dry period, restrict ventilation to increase humidity levels and mist the enclosure at least once a day. If males start calling in subsequent weeks they can be moved to a rain chamber, followed by females.

Tomato frogs lay hundreds of eggs in water, and these begin to hatch in less than two days. Tadpoles can be fed flake fish food. When they emerge from the water their coloration is not red, but dark gray and tan. Red begins to develop several months following metamorphosis.

## Marbled and Ornate Madascar Hoppers

Small and pudgy, *Scaphiophryne* species are exported seasonally from Madagascar for the pet trade. They are round, secretive frogs, maturing at around 1.5 inches (3.8 cm). The marbled hopper (*S. marmorata*) is most often found for sale. Camouflaged in bumpy moss green and brown, marbled hoppers are known only from a small area of eastern Madagascar rainforest. Another species occasionally seen is the ornate hopper (*S. gottlebei*), an unmistakably stunning amphibian. Also known as the rainbow burrowing frog, it is patterned in pink, green, and white, outlined by thick black borders. The ornate hopper is restricted to a small area of sandstone canyons in arid southwest Madagascar and is one of the island's most endangered amphibians.

In captivity, marbled hoppers have proven hardy and are fairly undemanding in care. Provide a loose substrate of coconut husk fiber and leaf litter to allow

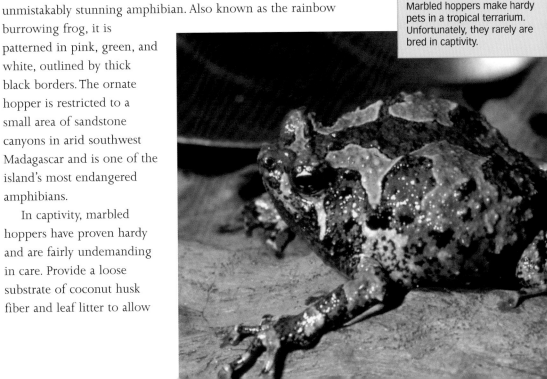

Marbled hoppers make hardy pets in a tropical terrarium. Unfortunately, they rarely are bred in captivity.

The beautiful ornate hopper lives in arid canyons in southwestern Madagascar. They require a fairly dry substrate when kept in the terrarium.

burrowing, as well as several plants and pieces of driftwood for the occasional nighttime climb. A small shallow water dish should also be available. Maintain tropical humidity levels much of the year through light daily mistings, accompanied by temperatures between 70° and 80°F (21° and 26.7°C). The ornate hopper comes from an arid environment and should be maintained on a somewhat dryer substrate, but otherwise its care is like that of the marbled hopper. Take care to monitor the moisture content of the substrate and ideally provide a gradient within it so that one end stays dryer than the other.

Much of the time *Scaphiophryne* remain hidden from view, and only occasionally do they venture out of hiding. Small crickets, flightless fruit flies, and other little invertebrates should be offered as food every other day, coated lightly in nutritional supplements.

There are few reports of *Scaphiophryne* species being bred in captivity. They are extremely explosive breeders in the wild, stimulated by heavy rains following an extended dry winter. In captivity, seasonal cycling, simulated rains, and an increase in available water could

## Responsible Hopper Keeping

**Although highly desirable due to its attractive appearance, the ornate hopper should only be kept in captivity as part of an organized breeding program. Its endangered status makes it inappropriate for keeping just as a pet.**

trigger a breeding response. Males are slightly smaller than females and call. Hundreds of eggs are laid on the water's surface and develop into tadpoles that feed on detritus and particles in the water column.

## Asian Painted Frog

Also regularly called the chubby frog or Asian bullfrog, the painted frog (*Kaloula pulchra*) is native to Southeast Asia, where it is common around human settlements and nearby forests. Adults measure between 2.1 inches (5.3 cm) and 3 inches (7.6 cm), and typically are patterned with two tan bands running down the back, in between which the color is dark brown. Asian painted frogs have large toe pads and are capable of climbing trees, though in captivity they usually remain in the lower half of the terrarium. Like tomato frogs, Asian painted frogs also produce a sticky white toxin when repeatedly harassed, so it is best to avoid handling this species.

Although mostly terrestrial, Asian painted frogs have sticky toe pads much like those of a tree frog and are able to climb trees.

# Look but Don't Touch

Asian painted frogs are enjoyable to watch at night as they cautiously walk around the cage to search for food. All individuals in the pet trade are wild caught, so carefully inspect frogs for signs of poor health before purchase. Cage setup is much like that for the tomato frog. Provide a loose substrate in which they can burrow, a shallow water dish, and hide spots. The temperature in the enclosure should remain warm, around 76°F (24.4°C), and can be accompanied by high levels of humidity between 60 and 100 percent.

Wild Asian painted frogs seem to prefer small foods like ants, but in captivity they readily accept crickets and other commercially available prey. Small crickets can be fed every other day, with other foods like flightless fruit flies or worms being substituted for crickets periodically. Use appropriate calcium and multivitamin supplements on food every other feeding.

Asian painted frogs are explosive breeders and can be found in large numbers floating in temporary pools of water that form during the monsoon season, but breeding rarely occurs in captivity. If attempting to breed this species in captivity, flooding the enclosure with water and misting heavily following a dry period of several months might induce breeding. Males have a particularly loud call that sounds a lot like a cow's moo. Many hundreds of eggs are laid on the surface of the water and hatch into tiny black tadpoles. These develop quickly, feeding on finely ground fish flakes and pellet foods.

## Crevice Creepers

Found for sale under numerous names, such as red-banded crevice creeper, red-banded rubber frog, and fire walking frog, Phrynomantis bifasciatus and P. microps are both attractively patterned in red and black. P. bifasciatus is larger, to 3 inches (7.6 cm) and has a set of two broken red stripes running down the dorsum. P. microps grows closer to 2 inches (5.1 cm) and has an entirely red or orange back. Both species have a large range in Africa, where they inhabit grasslands, savannahs, and agricultural areas, often being found near termite mounds or ant hills.

Crevice creepers are regularly imported for the pet trade, but few attempts to seriously keep and breed these species in captivity have been made by hobbyists or zoological institutions. A 10-gallon (38-l) aquarium is large enough for three. Use a substrate that allows frogs to dig under cage items, such as coconut husk fiber or sphagnum moss. Avoid wet conditions unless trying to induce breeding. Crevice creepers often are found in dry areas, and the moisture content of the substrate should reflect this. Provide a small, shallow dish of water and several pieces of cork bark or driftwood to create moist microclimates. Frogs may also use cage items for climbing at night. Maintain a temperature around 80°F (26.7°C), along with average household humidity levels that are temporarily increased by lightly misting the enclosure every couple of days. Crevice creepers feed on small crickets and other appropriately-sized food items.

Male *P. bifasciatus* may be smaller than females by half an inch (1.2 cm) and call with a musical trill. Breeding in the wild occurs during the rainy season, when large numbers of frogs congregate in temporary pools of water at night. They lay eggs around floating vegetation or on the water's surface, producing several hundred to 1,500. Tadpoles hatch after four days and filter feed on suspended food in the water column. In captivity, breeding could likely be achieved by putting frogs through a dry period of several months, followed by an increase in moisture and food availability, and finally a move to the rain chamber once males start to call.

## Running Frogs

Two *Kassina* species—usually called running frogs—are imported from Africa, where they inhabit savannahs, grasslands, and agricultural fields. The red-legged or spotted running frog (*Kassina maculata*) grows to 2.7 inches (6.8 cm) and is patterned in elegant chocolate spots laid over a gray-brown dorsal coloration. Red flash marks are found at the insertion of the limbs. The Senegal running frog (*K. senegalensis*) is smaller, to 2 inches (5.1 cm) at most, and is largely grayish tan with elongated spots or stripes down the back. Both are

*P. bifasciatus* (left) and *P. microps* (right) are sometimes confused in the pet trade. Their care is identical, although *P. bifasciatus* gets quite a bit larger than *P. microps*.

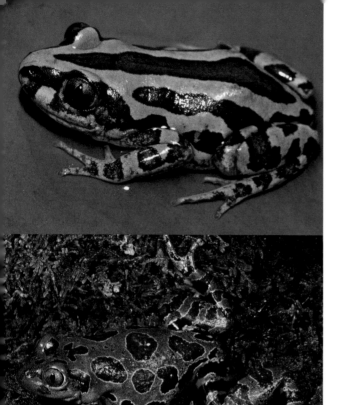

hardy amphibians, though they can be shy in captivity.

A 15-gallon (56.8-l) aquarium offers enough space for three adults. Use a substrate of moist sphagnum moss or coconut husk fiber, and submerge a large water dish in this substrate so that the rim is flush with the surface. Captive running frogs soak in this nightly. They are excellent climbers, and while running frogs often remain hidden during the day, at night they regularly venture up plants, driftwood, and other cage items. Offer crickets every other night, with foods like worms being substituted for crickets every few feedings. Running frogs should be kept between 70° and 78°F (21.1° and 25.6°C). Lightly mist the enclosure each night to provide increases in humidity that stimulate activity.

Male running frogs are slightly smaller than females and are vocal. If breeding is the goal, condition frogs with a cool dry period for one or two months, and then increase moisture, temperature, and food availability. If males begin to call, move them to a rain chamber outfitted with plenty of aquatic vegetation, which is where the females will lay eggs. Females should be introduced when they look swollen with eggs, and they may produce as many as 400 at once. Tadpoles are surprisingly large, growing bigger than adult frogs. Metamorphosis is completed in two to three months.

**top**: Despite its common name, the Senegal running frog is found over much of sub-Saharan Africa.
**bottom**: The red coloration at the base of the limbs of the spotted running frog is thought to startle predators when the frog hops away.

# Mantella Frogs

The genus *Mantella* is endemic to Madagascar and contains 16 recognized species, many of which display eye-catching colors to show they are poisonous. All are small frogs that measure around 1 inch (2.5 cm). Because they are both diurnal and colorful, mantellas are popular terrarium inhabitants. The golden mantella (*M. aurantiaca*), painted mantellas (*M. baroni* and *M. madagascariensis*), brown mantella (*M. ebenaui*), climbing mantella (*M. laevigata*), and green mantella (*M. viridis*) are most familiar to the pet trade.

Wild populations of many mantellas are endangered, and collection of frogs for the pet trade has put pressure on species already suffering from other threats like habitat loss. To locate a mantella breeder, check Internet classifieds on hobbyist websites and talk to other amphibian enthusiasts at reptile shows. Mantellas available from pet stores and dealers are most often wild caught.

Mantellas are best kept in large groups of the same species. A 20-gallon (75.7-l) aquarium offers enough space for six to eight frogs. Living terrariums as described in Chapter 2 are perfect, though mantellas can also do well in simpler setups with a substrate of sphagnum moss, a shallow water dish, and several plants. Males regularly call back and forth, with males of some species even wrestling each other over territory. Provide plenty of visual barriers and hide spots to avoid dominant individuals from stressing weaker ones.

The golden mantella occurs in the typical golden phase (left) as well as a more rarely seen ruby phase (right). This golden specimen is a gravid female; the outlines of several eggs are visible in her abdomen.

A temperature range between 65° and 75°F (18.3° and 24°C) is adequate for most species. Some mantellas, like the blue-legged mantella (M. expectata) and climbing mantella (M. laevigata), fare best when kept warmer, with part of the enclosure reaching 80°F (26.7°C) during the day. Others, such as the golden mantella (M. aurantiaca) and yellow mantella (M. crocea), are heat-sensitive, and extended exposure to warm temperatures can prove fatal. Offer high levels of humidity (70 to 100 percent). This can be accomplished by restricting ventilation to a third or less of a screen cover and misting the enclosure daily.

The blue-legged mantella is critically endangered in nature. Habitat loss is the biggest threat to its survival.

Provide captive mantellas with a diet of small crickets, flightless fruit flies, springtails, small wax worms, and other appropriately sized food items. Offer food every other day for adults, coating it in a nutritional supplement at least every other feeding.

A cool, dry winter is necessary to condition mantellas to breed. Keep frogs below 72°F (22.2°C) for several months and mist the enclosure only weekly. Exposed to these harsh conditions, mantellas seek shelter in damp areas to conserve moisture. Following a

Mantella baroni is one of the most common mantellas in captivity. It was formerly imported under the name M. madagascariensis, a similarly patterned species.

cool period, bring temperatures back to normal, mist the enclosure several times each day, and feed heavily. They lay eggs on land, often concealed under a piece of bark or buried in little pockets of moist moss. The ovum is white. Clutch size varies with species, but commonly numbers between 40 and 80. In nature, annual flooding sweeps the tadpoles into the water, but in the terrarium the keeper has to do this. Move the eggs to a separate container with shallow water (about 0.20 inches [0.5 cm]) once development in eggs can be seen.

## Caring Parents

*Mantella laevigata* breeds in a different way than the rest of the genus. Tadpoles mature in small pools of water, often above ground in tree hollows, with the mother feeding infertile eggs to them while they grow. In the terrarium, film canisters and sections of bamboo are popular egg deposition sites. Position angled or vertical film canisters partially filled with water in the upper parts of the terrarium, or use pieces of bamboo 2 to 4 inches (5.1 to 10.2 cm) in diameter, filled with a little water, and placed standing upright to form breeding sites.

Tadpoles actively feed on algae and fish flakes and take two to four months to complete metamorphosis. Newly metamorphosed mantellas measure less than 0.4 inches (1.0 cm), and must be fed springtails and pinhead crickets until they are old enough to eat larger foods. It may take some species one year to reach full adult coloration.

## Vietnamese Mossy Frog

One of the most exciting frogs to enter the pet trade in recent years is the Vietnamese mossy frog (*Theloderma corticale*). These frogs are unusual amphibians, camouflaged in green and red tubercles to mimic moss. When disturbed they may roll into a ball and play dead. Adult females grow to 3.3 inches (8.4 cm); males stay smaller, near 2.4 inches (6.1 cm). Mossy frogs inhabit rocky cliffs in rainforests of northern Vietnam.

Thanks to captive-breeding efforts, Vietnamese mossy frogs can be found for sale at reptile shows and specialty pet stores. They make hardy captives when kept in the appropriate environment. A standard 20-gallon (75.7-l) aquarium is large enough for three adults. Mossy frogs are semi-aquatic and live near rocky water-filled crevices or streams, so the enclosure must incorporate a large area of water. A setup similar to that for fire-bellied toads (*Bombina* spp.) works well, though because they have enlarged toe pads and are good climbers, they should be provided with plenty of plants and wood for climbing at night. Filter water with a small submersible power filter.

Provide a temperature range between 75° and 86°F (24° and 30°C) during the day, dropping to about 72°F (22.2°C) at night. Accompany these warm temperatures with high levels of humidity.

Crickets form the bulk of a mossy frog diet. Roaches, worms, and house flies can be mixed in for variety. It may be helpful to use a feeding dish to prevent prey from drowning. Offer food to adults twice a week and to juveniles every night, coated with nutritional supplements.

Vietnamese mossy frogs (adult on left and tailed froglet on right) are relatively easy to breed and are produced in good numbers. It takes about three weeks for the tadpoles to turn into frogs.

Breeding mossy frogs is not difficult. Frogs should be conditioned with a cool period of two months during which temperatures stay between 55° and 68°F (12.8° and 20°C). Once the frogs are returned to normal conditions males begin calling, and if females are responsive they call back. Eggs (often less than a dozen) are deposited overhanging the water. Many breeders use ceramic flower pots for egg deposition sites, but mossy frogs also have been known to deposit eggs on plants or rocks near water. Leave eggs in the enclosure until they hatch, which takes one to two weeks. Move the tadpoles to their own enclosure. Tadpoles feed well on fish foods, and at a water temperature of 77°F (25°C) they take around three months to complete metamorphosis.

## Other Mossy Frogs

A handful of other interesting *Theloderma* species have entered the trade, and frog breeders are starting to produce them. *Theloderma asperum*, the pied warty frog, is a particularly interesting and hardy one. They are small, growing only to 1.5 inches (3.7 cm) and are colored in contrasting gray and white, mimicking bird droppings. Keep them in a semi-aquatic setup with plenty of rocks, cork bark tubes, and other objects protruding from the water area. Natural fluctuations in household temperature and humidity in combination with water changes easily spark breeding behavior, with eggs being laid on land in small clutches of around a half dozen.

Other species, such as *T. stellatum* and *T. bicolor*, also have recently made an appearance in the pet trade. Care and breeding techniques for these two tree hole-dwelling anurans are still being worked out.

## Malaysian Leaf Frog

Well disguised as a dead leaf, the Malaysian leaf frog (*Megophrys nasuta*) blends into the tropical forest floors of Thailand, Malaysia, and Indonesia. Females are massive, capable of growing to 7.3 inches (18.5 cm), while males are only half this size. Long fleshy horns protrude over the eyes and snout and a pattern of browns coats the body. Wild-caught animals are imported with some frequency, and you will most easily find them at reptile shows or through dealers.

The short-horned leaf frog (*Xenophrys* [*Megophrys*] *aceras*) and dwarf Malaysian leaf frog (*Megophrys montana*) are also sometimes available. Both are smaller than *M. nasuta*, with *X. aceras* growing between 1.9 and 3.4 inches (4.8 and 8.6 cm) and large female *M. montana* reaching at

Malaysian leaf frogs often fail to acclimate to captivity and are rarely captive bred. These frogs are best left to experienced keepers.

most 4.4 inches (11.1 cm). Care for both of these seldom-seen leaf frogs is like that for M. *nasuta*, though housing does not need to be as large.

While they are highly desirable to keep because of their exotic appearance, Malaysian leaf frogs prove troublesome to acclimate to captivity and are best left to experienced keepers. Keepers should initially house frogs individually in simple setups lined with moist paper towels, several easily cleaned hide spots, and a water dish. Parasite and bacterial infections are not uncommon, so maintain high levels of cleanliness and consult a veterinarian in advance of acquiring frogs.

Once their health is assured, you can move Malaysian leaf frogs to larger, more natural enclosures. A 30-gallon (113.6-l) aquarium provides enough space for two or three. The enclosure can be lined with coconut husk fiber, sphagnum moss, or a mixture of ingredients. Offer a large water dish up to 3 inches (7.6 cm) deep, as well as curled pieces of cork bark or driftwood for hiding. Temperatures should stay between 70° and 78°F (21.1° and 25.6°C), along with a humidity level around 75 percent. The usual fare of large invertebrates, including crickets, cockroaches and worms, makes a good diet. Feed three to six food items per frog every other day.

Breeding is rarely achieved in captivity. Females can be difficult to obtain and usually fetch a higher price than the smaller, vocal males. Cool the cage to around 72°F (22.2°C) and reduce misting frequency to condition frogs for breeding. After one month, bring frogs back to normal temperatures, feed heavily, and mist multiple times daily.

Leaf frogs are stream breeders and attach eggs to objects bordering moving water. In captivity, slabs of cork bark along the water's edge are often used. As many as 1,400 eggs make up a clutch, though they are not always laid together at the same time. Tadpoles have interesting upturned mouths and surface-feed on floating foods. Maintain a water temperature near 77°F (25°C). At around three months the first frogs leave the water, though some individuals take considerably longer to morph out. Juveniles resemble adults but are tiny and must be fed hatchling crickets and fruit flies.

## Solomon Islands Leaf Frog

Another leaf mimic occasionally encountered at pet stores and reptile shows is *Ceratobatrachus guentheri*, the Solomon Islands leaf frog or eyelash frog. This frog closely

**top**: Superficially similar to the Malaysian leaf frog, the Solomon Islands leaf frog is not closely related. They are somewhat difficult to acclimate to captivity.
**bottom**: Clutch of Solomon Islands leaf frog eggs. The young pass through the tadpole stage within the egg, hatching out as tiny frogs.

resembles a leaf when viewed from above, with pointed projections over each eye, the snout, and leg joints. Coloration is variable. Brown and rust-colored individuals are most commonly encountered, but mossy green, white, orange, and golden Solomon Islands leaf frogs also show up in the mix. They can reach 3.4 inches (8.6 cm) in length, with females being slightly larger than males. Size is the best way to sex leaf frogs, because both males and females are vocal.

Once acclimated, Solomon Islands leaf frogs make fine captives. Unfortunately, wild-caught frogs can have difficulty adjusting to captivity. Use a simple large setup for newly imported leaf frogs, and monitor them for signs of parasite and bacterial infections. Because of their powerful hind limbs, the pointed projections on the head of leaf frogs sometimes are rubbed down from continually trying to escape small enclosures. A saline solution or topical antibiotic ointment should be applied to these wounds if present when acquired. Captive-bred *C. guentheri* are usually problem-free, and if available should be chosen over wild-caught animals.

A group of three adult frogs can be maintained in a 20-gallon (75.7-l) aquarium. Use a substrate that allows frogs to burrow, such as sphagnum moss or coconut husk fiber. These leaf frogs are ambush predators, much like horned frogs (*Ceratophrys* spp.), and appreciate cover. Cork bark, driftwood, and artificial plants are all good options. The temperature during the day should range from 74° to 86°F (23.3° to 30°C), with high levels of humidity (around 75 percent) accompanying these warm temperatures. Crickets form a good staple diet. Mix in night crawlers, leaf worms, super worms, and an occasional pinky mouse for variety. Note that leaf frogs will eat other frogs and should not be housed with smaller individuals.

Breeding Solomon Islands leaf frogs in captivity is possible, but it only occasionally occurs. This is unfortunate, because they have a fascinating reproductive strategy. Eggs are deposited in a small hole and then buried. Larvae undergo direct development, and transform into miniature leaf frogs within the egg after one month. Most often 30 to 40 eggs are laid and sometimes go unnoticed in the terrarium until baby frogs are found hopping about. To induce breeding, increase the available moisture and humidity by misting the cage frequently.

Heavily fed females produce eggs, which can be seen through the sides of the body before they are laid. Monitor females to determine whether eggs have been buried in the enclosure. If eggs are found, remove them with the surrounding soil to a container for incubation. Once frogs hatch they can be housed in groups of 10 to 15 in 10-gallon (38-l) aquariums under similar conditions as adults.

## Rice Paddy Floating Frog

More often found for sale in the fish department than the herp department of pet stores, the rice paddy floating frog (Occidozyga lima) makes an enjoyable captive. They are small, maturing at only around 1.0 inch (2.5 cm) in length. Often a light dorsal stripe runs down their gray-brown to olive-colored body. Adapted to life on the water's surface, floating frogs have eyes on top of their head and heavily webbed feet. They are widely distributed throughout southern Asia where they spend time in areas with still or slow-moving water. Available exclusively at this time as wild-caught stock, floating frogs are regularly housed in

Small and hardy, rice paddy floating frogs make hardy and unusual pets. They only come onto land occasionally.

Unidentified *Occidozyga* species from Indonesia floating on the water's surface as is typical for all the frogs in this genus.

crowded conditions at dealers, so be sure to inspect their health carefully before purchase.

A standard 10-gallon aquarium (38-l) is adequate space for four adult frogs. Fill the aquarium with around 3.0 inches (7.6 cm) of water and include floating and emergent vegetation for floating frogs to rest on. A large stone or piece of cork bark should also be offered, not only to provide a small area out of water for the frogs, but also to help prevent feeder insects from drowning. Weekly water changes will maintain water quality. If filtration is used, diffuse the output so there is little to no current. Small crickets form a good staple diet, being offered every other day, with other foods such as live blackworms (placed in small globs on land) or flightless fruit flies being substituted for crickets periodically.

Floating frogs can be sexed when examined in a group. Males are normally smaller and develop nuptial pads when conditioned to breed. Presumably an increase in temperature, humidity, and water level could trigger breeding in captivity, but there are no reliable documented accounts of this occurring. Tadpoles of several other *Occidozyga* species are predatory, feeding on tiny aquatic invertebrates, and this may hold true of *O. lima* as well.

*AmphibiaWeb*. Accessed 09 Nov. 2009. <http://www.amphibiaweb.org>.

"How to Recognise Chytrid Fungus." *Frog Decline Reversal Project*. Accessed 17 Nov. 2009. <http://www.fdrproject.org/pages/disease/CHYrecog.htm>.

Abate, Ardi. 2002. *Thoughts for Food*. 3rd ed. Chameleon Information Network.

Bartlett, Dick. 2002. "Two Fat Frogs." *Reptiles* 10(10): 30-40.

Bartlett, Dick. 2004. "A Who's Who of North American Toads." *Reptiles* 12(2):28-35.

Bartlett, Richard, and Patricia Bartlett. 2000. *The Horned Frog Family and the African Bullfrogs*. Danbury: Barron's Educational Series.

Bradley, Teresa A., and Kevin Wright. 2000. "Captive care and breeding of White's tree frog, *Pelodryas caerulea*." *Journal of Herpetological Medicine and Surgery* 10.2: 21-25.

Behler, John. 1979. *National Audubon Society Field Guide to Reptiles and Amphibians*. New York: Knopf: Distributed by Random House.

Candioti, M. F. Vera. 2005. "Morphology and feeding in tadpoles of *Ceratophrys cranwelli* (Anura: Leptodactylidae)." *Acta Zoologica* 86: 1-11.

Channing, A., L. Du Preez, and N. Passmore. 1994. "Status, vocalization and breeding biology of two species of African bullfrogs (Ranidae: Pyxicephalus)." *Journal of Zoology* 234: 141-148.

Clare, John. "African Bullfrog Care." *Frog Forum*. Accessed 10 Dec. 2009. <http://www.frogforum.net/frog-toad-care-sheets/Pyxicephalus-adspersus-Pyxie-Pyxi-African-Bullfrog-Giant-Frog-Care-Sheet-Info.html>.

Channing, Alan. 2001. *Amphibians of Central and Southern Africa*. Ithaca, NY: Cornell UP.

Cooper, Steve. 2002. "Red-Eyed Wonders." *Reptiles* 10(3): 28-35.

Daszak, P., A. Strieby, A. A. Cunningham, J. E. Longcore, C. C. Brown, and D. Porter. 2004. "Experimental evidence that the bullfrog (*Rana catesbeiana*) is a potential carrier of chytridiomycosis, an emerging fungal disease of amphibians." *Herpetological Journal* 14: 201-207.

Densmore, Christine and David Green. 2007. "Diseases of Amphibians." *ILAR Journal* 48(3): 235-254.

Duellman, William and Miguel Lizana. 1994. "Biology of a sit-and-wait predator, the Leptodactylid frog *Ceratophrys cornuta*." *Herpetologica* 50 (1): 51-64.

Edmonds, Les. 1992. "The Suriname Toad, *Pipa pipa*." *Tropical Fish Hobbyist* 40(6): 140-142.

Ferrier, Wayne. 1997. "Natural History and Captive Care of the American Bullfrog." *Reptile and Amphibian Magazine* 51: 38-43.

Frost, Darrel R. "Amphibian Species of the World: an Online Reference. Version 5.0." *American Museum of Natural History*. Accessed 24 Dec. 2009. <http://research.amnh.org/herpetology/amphibia/index.html>.

Hadfield, Catherine, and Brent Whitaker. 2005. "Amphibian emergency medicine and care." *Seminars in Avian and Exotic Pet Medicine* 14(2): 79-89.

Harkewicz, Kenneth. 2004. "Maintenance of *Bombina* species of frogs." *Seminars in Avian and Exotic Pet Medicine* 13(4): 229-233.

Harkewicz, Kenneth. 2006. "What's new in amphibian herpetoculture: care and breeding of several species new to the pet trade." *Proceedings of the Annual Conference of the Association of Reptile and Amphibian Veterinarians.* 13: 5-7.

Hunzlker, Ray. 1995. *Horned Frogs.* Neptune City, NJ: TFH Publications.

Irven, Paul. 1998. "West African dwarf clawed frogs *Hymenochirus curtipes*, breeding and husbandry in captivity." *Ratel* 25(2): 61-68.

Johnson, Megan, Lee Berger, Lara Philips, Richard Speare. 2003. "Fungicidal effects of chemical disinfectants, UV light, desiccation and heat on the amphibian chytrid *Batrachochytrium dendrobatidis*." *Disease of Aquatic Organisms* 57: 225-260.

Kowalski, Edward. 2004. "They Are What They Eat." *Reptiles* 12(8): 40-43.

Mazorlig, Tom. 1999. "Life with Eyelash Frogs." *Reptile and Amphibian Hobbyist* 4(9): 44-50.

Merker, Walter. 2010. "Camouflage Kings." *Reptiles* 18(1): 24-31.

Moore, Mary. 2001. "African Bullfrogs (*Pyxicephalus*), Their Natural History and Captive Care." *Reptile and Amphibian Hobbyist* 6(7): 18-23.

Ryboltovsky, Evgeny. 1999. "A Wonderful Frog From Vietnam: Biology, Management and Breeding." *International Zoo News*. Accessed 8 Feb. 2010. < http://www.zoonews.co.uk/IZN/295/IZN-295.html#frog>.

Schad, K., editor. Amphibian Population Management Guidelines. *Amphibian Ark Amphibian Population Management Workshop: 2007 December 10-11: San Diego, CA*, USA. Amphibian Ark. www.amphibianark.org: 2008.

Scherff-Norris, Kirsta, Lauren Livo, Allan Pessier, Craig Fetkavich, Mark Jones, Mark Kombert, Anna Goebel, and Brint Spencer. 2002. *Boreal Toad Husbandry Manual*. Colorado Division of Wildlife.

Sparreboom, Max and Paul Van Den Elzen. 1998. "Preliminary note on the care and breeding of *Bombina maxima* (Boulenger, 1905) in captivity." *British Herpetological Society Bulletin* 65.

Staniszewski, Marc. 1995. *Amphibians in Captivity.* Neptune City, NJ: T.F.H.

Staniszewski, Marc. "Marc Staniszewski's Bombina FAQ." *Amphibian Information Centre*. Accessed 02 Nov. 2009. <http://www.amphibian.co.uk/bombina.html>.

Tillson-Willis, Andrew. 2009. "Difficult Devil. Breeding Cranwell's Horned Frog is a Challenge." *Reptiles* 17 (1): 26-31.

Vosjoli, Philippe De. 1990. *Horned Frogs* (General Care and Maintenance of Series) Concord: Advanced Vivarium Systems.

Walls, Jerry. 2003. "Ask the Breeder: American Toads." *Reptiles* 11(6): 22.

Wilkinson, John. 1998. "Propagation of the Far Eastern (*Bombina orientalis*) and European fire-bellied toads (*Bombina bombina*) under captive conditions." *Advances in Amphibian Research in the Former Soviet Union* 3: 205-213.

Wise, Charles. 1993. "Send in the Clowns." *Tropical Fish Hobbyist* 41(7): 102-106.

Wright, Kevin. "Corneal Lipidosis." *Arizona Exotic Animal Hospital.* Accessed 08 Dec. 2009. <http://www.azeah.com/Care-Sheets.asp?id=176>.

Wright, Kevin. 2009. "Advances that impact every amphibian patient." *Exotic DVM* 7(3): 82-86.

Wright, Kevin and Brent Whitaker. 2001. *Amphibian Medicine and Captive Husbandry.* Krieger Publishing Company, Malabar, Florida.

Young, Bruce E., Simon N. Stuart, Janice S. Chanson, Neil A. Cox, and Timothy M. Boucher. 2004. *Disappearing Jewels: the Status of New World Amphibians.* Arlington, Virginia: NatureServe,

Yu Guohua, Junxing Yang, Mingwang Zhang, and Dingqu Rao. 2007. "Phylogenetic and systematic study of the genus *Bombina* (Amphia: Anura: Bombinatoridae): New insights from molecular data." *Journal of Herpetology* 41(3): 365-377.

Zippel, Kevin. 2006. "Further observations of oviposition in the Suriname Toad (*Pipa pipa*) with comments on biology, misconceptions, and husbandry." *Herpetological Review* 37(1): 60-68.

Zippel, Kevin. " Water Quality and Filtration for Amphibians. " Accessed 13 Nov. 2009. <http://home.att.net/~kczippel/waterqual.html>.

# Resources
## Clubs and Societies

American Society of Ichthyologists and Herpetologists
Maureen Donnelly, Secretary
Florida International University
Biological Sciences
11200 SW 8th St.
Miami, FL 33199
Phone: 305-348-1235
Fax: 305-348-4172
E-mail: maureen.a.donnelly@gmail.com
www.asih.org

Society for the Study of Amphibians and Reptiles (SSAR)
Marion Preest, Secretary
Joint Science Department
The Claremont Colleges
925 N. Mills Ave.
Claremont, CA 91711
Phone: 909-607-8014
Fax: 909-621-8588
E-mail: mpreest@jsd.claremont.edu
www.ssarherps.org

## Veterinary Resources

Association of Reptile and Amphibian Veterinarians
810 East 10th
PO Box 1897
Lawrence, KS 66044
Phone: 800-6270326
Fax: 785-843-6153
www.arav.org

## Websites

### Amphibian Conservation

Amphibian Specialist Group
www.amphibians.org

Amphibian Ark
www.amphibianark.org

Partners in Amphibian and Reptile Conservation (PARC)
www.parcplace.org

Project Golden Frog
www.ranadorada.org

Save a Frog
www.saveafrog.org

Tree Walkers International
www.treewalkers.org

### Amphibian Information

Amphibiancare.com (author's site)
www.amphibiancare.com/frogs/main.html

Amphibian Species of the World Online Reference
Research.amnh.org/vz/herpetology/amphibia

Froggie.info
www.froggie.info

Frogland
allaboutfrogs.org

The Kapok Tree
www.freewebs.com/kapoktree/

Living Underworld: Amphibian Information Resource
www.livingunderworld.org

Marc Staniszweski's Amphibian Information Centre
www.amphibian.co.uk

### General Herp Information

Center for North American Herpetology
www.cnah.org

Herp Digest
www.herpdigest.org

Kingsnake.com
www.kingsnake.com

Melissa Kaplan's Herp Care Collection
www.anapsid.org

Reptile Forums
www.reptileforums.com

The Reptile Rooms
www.reptilerooms.com

## Books

Edmonds, Devin. *Newts and Salamanders.* T.F.H. Publications, Inc.

Edmonds, Devin. *Tree Frogs.* T.F.H. Publications, Inc.

Hellweg, Michael R. *Raising Live Foods.* T.F.H. Publications, Inc.

Purser, Philip. *Natural Terrariums*. T.F.H. Publications, Inc.

Sihler, Amanda and Greg Sihler. *Poison Dart Frogs*. T.F.H. Publications, Inc.

## Magazines

*Reptiles* Magazine
PO Box 6050
Mission Viejo, CA 92690
www.reptilechannel.com/reptile-magazines/reptiles-magazine/default.aspx

*Reptilia* Magazine
Bisbe Urquinaona 34
08860 Castelldefels
Barcelona
Spain
subscriptions@reptilia.net
www.reptilia.net

## About the Author:

Devin Edmonds lives in Madison, Wisconsin and has kept frogs and toads since childhood. He maintains a popular website about their care (www.amphibiancare.com) and is currently working on an amphibian conservation project with Association Mitsinjo, an organization in Madagascar, and the Wildlife Conservation Society.

Alslutsky (courtesy of Shutterstock): 142 (left)

Randall D. Babb: 98

Marian Bacon: 4, 95, 119, 132, 134

R.D. Bartlett: 70, 75 (top), 82, 83, 97, 139 (right), 146

Cindy Bensaid: 125 127 (top), 128, 129

Ryan M. Boltan (courtesy of Shutterstock): 49, 109, 116

Allen Both: 12, 34, 40, 76, 78, 86

Steve Bower (courtesy of Shutterstock): 56

Jon Boxall: 104

Magdalena Bujak (courtesy of Shutterstock): 93

Marius Burger: 138 (top)

Sascha Burkard (courtesy of Shutterstock): front cover

P. Donovan: 36

EcoPrint (courtesy of Shutterstock): 88

Devin Edmonds: 14, 16, 22, 23, 26, 28, 30, 31, 32, 33, 50, 52, 53, 54, 55, 96, 114, 139 (left), 142 (right)

Paul Freed: 58, 65, 87, 106 (right), 117, 140 (top), 145 (bottom), 147

U. E. Friese: 21

James Gerholdt: 62

Michael Gilroy: 92 (bottom)

Charles Harrison: 42 (left)

Michael R. Hellweg: 42 (right)

D. and K. Kucharscy (courtesy of Shutterstock): 1

Jerry R. Loll: 89

Erik Loza: 138 (bottom)

G. and C. Merker: 110, 130, 143

G. and Walter Merker: 66

Jason Mintzer (courtesy of Shutterstock): 99

John C. Murphy: 118

Aaron Norman: 6, 73, 80 (left), 106 (left), 124, 127 (bottom)

Mark Smith: 94, 120, 133, and back cover

Marc S. Staniszewski: 10, 38, 64

Karl H. Switak: 8, 44, 47, 60, 69, 75 (center), 80 (right), 81, 85, 92 (top), 100, 102, 105, 112, 115, 137, 140 (bottom)

Angela M. Thomas: 75 (bottom)

Fekete Tibor (courtesy of Shutterstock): 113

Birute Vijeikiene (courtesy of Shutterstock): 108

Maleta M. Walls: 145 (top)

Pan Xunbin (courtesy of Shutterstock): 135

Frank B. Yuwono (courtesy of Shutterstock): 90

# OTHER TITLES IN THE COMPLETE HERP CARE SERIES

Newts and Salamanders
(ISBN: 978-0-7938-2899-9)

Poison Dart Frogs
(ISBN: 978-0-7938-28937)

Tree Frogs
(ISBN: 978-0-7938-2894-4)

Aquatic Turtles (ISBN: 978-0-7938-2885-2)

Ball Pythons (ISBN: 978-0-7938

Bearded Dragons (ISBN: 978-0-793

Box Turtles (ISBN: 978-0-7938-

Corn and Rat Snakes (ISBN: 978-0-79

Crested Geckos (ISBN: 978-0-793

Green Iguanas (ISBN: 978-0-7938

Insect-Eating Lizards (ISBN: 978-0-7

King and Milk Snakes (ISBN: 978-0-79

Leopard Geckos (ISBN: 978-0-793

Natural Terrariums (ISBN: 978-0-79

Raising Live Foods (ISBN: 978-0-793

Red-Tailed Boas (ISBN: 978-0-7938

Russian Tortoises (ISBN: 978-0-793

Savannah Monitors (ISBN: 978-0-793

Sulcata and Leopard Tortoises (ISBN: 978-0-7938-2898-2)

Uromastyx (ISBN: 978-0-7938-2897-5)

Water Dragons (ISBN: 978-0-7938-2884-5)